To Jay!
love + enjoy,
Nancy M.

BUILT TO GRIND

�֎ ✖ ✖ ✖ **25 YEARS** of hardcore skateboarding

from the archives of

INDEPENDENT
TRUCK COMPANY

Editor
Bob Denike

Photo Editor / Associate Editor
Bryce Kanights

Art Director / Designer
Johnny "Mojo" Munnerlyn

Managing Editor
Keith Wilson

Executive Copy Editor
Annie Tucker

Project Consultant
Joseph Tershay

Production Artist
Kristine MacAulay

Contributing Photographers
Jerry Alba, Liz Alba, Steve Alba, Desiree R. Astorga, Michael Blabac, Florian Böhm, Jaya Bonderov, Dan Bourqui, Brad Bowman, J. Grant Brittain, Joe Brook, Michael Burnett, Thomas Campbell, Reg Caselli, James Cassimus, Greg Cespedes, Lance Dalgart, Lance Dawes, Michael Derewenko, Ed Dominick, Matt Etheridge, Craig Fineman, Mörizen Foche, Morgan Ghan, Bill Golding, Jim Goodrich, Joe Hammeke, Theo Hand, Jon Humphries, Spike Jonze, Bryce Kanights, Randy Katen, Chuck Katz, Steve Keenan, Jeff Kendall, Brendan Klein, Jim Knight, Rick Kosick, John Krisick, Jon Malvino, Andrew Mapstone, Larry Marshall, Dennis McGrath, Gary Mederios, Cesario "Block" Montaño, Gabe Morford, Jody Morris, John Myers, Pat Myers, Scott Needham, Jeff Newton, Tsuyoshi Nishiyama, Richard Novak, Mark Oblow, Patrick O'Dell, Luke Ogden, James O'Mahoney, Chris Ortiz, Tim Piumarta, Ed Riggins, Chris "Rhino" Rooney, Rich Rose, Nick Scurich, Aaron Sedway, Keith Stephenson, Tod Swank, Dave Swift, Jai Tanju, Ted Terrebonne, Joseph Tershay, Kevin J. Thatcher, Bill Thomas, Tony Vitello, Miki Vuckovich, Mark Whiteley, Tobin Yelland, Steve Zirwas

Contributing Writers
Steve Alba, Tony Alva, Ray Barbee, Rick Blackhart, Brad Bowman, Brian Brannon, Steve Caballero, Mary Carver, Chet Childress, Lance Dawes, Bob Denike, John Dettman-Lytle, Dave Dominy, Dave Duncan, Skip Engblom, Mörizen Foche, Scott Foss, Peter Gifford, Mike Goldman, Mark Gonzales, Jeff Grosso, Joe Hammeke, Steve Harding, Tony Hawk, Curtis Hesslegrave, Henry Hester, Jimmy Hoffman, Christian Hosoi, Ivan Hosoi, Jerry "Taters" Hurtado, John Hutson, Bryce Kanights, Tom Knox, John Krisik, Jason Lee, John Lucero, Dave McIntyre, Aaron Meza, Cesario "Block" Montaño, D. David Morin, Lance Mountain, Richard Novak, Gavin O'Brien, Steve Olson, Judi Oyama, Al Partanen, Duane Peters, Jim Phillips, Tim Piumarta, John Politis, Eddie Reategui, Justin Regan, Ed Riggins, Tony Roderick, John Solimine, C.R. Stecyk III, Eric Swenson, Joseph Tershay, Kevin J. Thatcher, Jim Thiebaud, Fausto Vitello, Damon Way, Mark Whiteley, Keith Wilson

Special Thanks
All past and present NHS and Ermico employees, skateboarders, skateshops, and distributors worldwide, Mark Widmann, Jeff Kendall, Ed Riggins, Michael McDaniel, Tim Butler, Craig Stecyk, Dave McIntyre

Scans by Scott Kennedy and Mike Miller
Prism Photographics Inc., Santa Cruz, CA

BUILT TO GRIND
25 YEARS OF HARDCORE SKATEBOARDING
FROM THE ARCHIVES OF INDEPENDENT TRUCK COMPANY

Authored in 2004 by NHS, Inc.
Published exclusively for NHS, Inc. by High Speed Productions, Inc.

Skateboard Shops and International Distributors contact:
NHS, Inc. 831.459.7800
PO Box 2718, Santa Cruz, CA 95063
www.independenttrucks.com
www.builttogrind.com

Booksellers in the USA contact:
High Speed Productions, Inc. 415.671.2413
1303 Underwood Avenue, San Francisco, CA 94124

FIRST EDITION

ISBN 0-9657271-8-1
Library of Congress Control Number: 2004101318

BUILT TO GRIND �҂ ✚ ✚ ✚
contents

Left: *Armed with a fistful of attitude, Peter Gifford commandeers a frontside arc at Spinning Wheels Skatepark, Cupertino, CA, February 1979. Cover: Skatespots come and go, but a loud and long frontside grind is forever. Tony Trujillo lays down a timeless Smith grind in Tahoe City, CA, 2003.*

An Independent Truck Company baseplate casting (often referred to as a "tree,") prior to cutting, grinding, drilling, tumbling, and assembly.

This book is based on the recollections of many. Due mainly to the altered states of all parties involved, some agree, others don't, and some simply can't remember. While some are stoked, others are jaded, and a few just don't give a damn. One thing is solid: the main characters were in the same places, at the same times, and for the same events, yet they all walked away with a slightly different perspective. So be it. That's Independent. —B.D.

Old Was Out and New Was In —It Was Time to Turn

By C.R. Stecyk III

Twenty-five years of Independent Truck Company constitutes an anniversary that demands both respect and introspection. The contemporary tendency is to envelop history in an impenetrable containment sphere of numeric details. The human relevance of occurrences and entities becomes lost in a blizzard of data. What real consequence do computations of ballistic rounds expended, X billion burgers served, acres burned, number of units produced, pool size of participants, topographical chart coordinates, revenues generated, reentry duration times, calories used, et cetera, have? What stats could convey the impact of 25 years of Independent?

The value of Independent far exceeds its performance as a business entity. Granted, Independent Trucks are the de facto standard of contemporary skateboard truck design. Virtually all legendary riders have been associated with Independent in some way at some time. No professional skateboarder or company owner exists who is not aware of the Independent hegemony. Nevertheless, the true accomplishment here is about people and their discovery of a workable way to live out their lives. Whatever success they ultimately garnered is incidental to that first pure impulse. Independent is proof that the hectic will inevitably push out the hype. The Independent Trucks cartel is very much a family. Once you are in, you are never out.

Every person in this narrative is more or less connected to the others. That interrelation and the expectation of excellence are the primary mechanisms that drive the beast known as Independent. It has always been about the truck.

Webster's Unabridged Dictionary *describes the truck as "a wheeled vehicle consisting of a frame with a pair of wheels to carry and guide one end of a vehicle in turning sharp turns." Independent is defined as "not dependent; not subject to control by others, not affiliated; not looking to others for one's opinions or for guidance in conduct."*

Certainly, there were trucks before Independent. Petitbled patented the first inline roller skate in 1819. James Plimpton brought out the quad roller skate in 1863. Chicago and Sure Grip shoe skates were fixtures in the market from the 1930s on. Sidewalk surfers used to find those clunkers, cut them down, and separate the trucks. Mark Richards was a skater from North Hollywood, California who had the hubris to call up the Chicago Roller Skate Company and suggest that they sell him separate trucks on mounting plates. It took the midwestern roller rink businessmen months to understand what he was getting at, but they finally relented, and the first designated skateboard truck came to the bazaar. This brilliantly simple move in 1963 helped permanently establish Richards' fledgling Val Surf as an industry leader.

By the '70s, trucks were beginning to be made with other specific skateboard-centric design attributes. Mr. Bennett sold trucks out of his Rolls Royce. The Bahne brothers made a truck. Dave Dominy created a wider truck for slalom called Tracker. Gull Wing die-cast their lot and used cooling fins that were highly reminiscent of 1930s Elgin bicycle hubs. These were the leading brands in a rapidly growing market. Others included Lazer, Excaliber, California Slalom, and ACS. The circus of skateboarding was well populated by a thousand other fly-by-night jokers, toy makers, and opportunists.

The skateboard was the logical conclusion to several millennia of evolutionary development. As a compact, scaled form of performance transportation that is highly efficient and is made of basically renewable/recyclable materials, the skateboard remains a viable paradigm for the future. It was horrifically telling that the industry of the period was, by and large, controlled by non-skating interlopers who had no true appreciation for the very phenomenon that supported them. Into the sanctimony of all this "fun in the sun and income too" boosterism came the nihilistic scourge of Independent Truck Company.

Events come and go with monotonous predictability. Early skateboard trials sucked dick because of their irrelevance. Most were staged by promoters who had no clue and couldn't have cared less about terrain. The '65 Anaheim, '75 Del Mar, and '78 Akron contest presentations all proved that marginal conditions prevent contestants from skating anywhere close to their fullest abilities. If the overriding goal was to provide visual fodder for the mainstream TV outlets, then in a sense, the three aforementioned contests succeeded. Generally, though, pandering to mass sensibility engenders mediocrity and stagnation.

Signal Hill's infamous downhill was steep and scary. From 1975 through 1978, these World Speed Championships, held on a treacherous slope near Long Beach, California, were the most uninhibited manifestation of skate competition ever.

Rules surrounding the matter were clear and concise: the fastest time on the clock won—no excuses, no worries, and no apologies. All comers were invited, and a number of names in the commercial sector avoided the gig like the plague. Careers and bodies were broken there, and James O'Mahoney, the *éminence grise* who organized this competition, cut whiners no slack. The diversity of

classes at the Hill was unprecedented, and in 1977, skate car and street luge disciplines were included with the regular stand-up classifications.

The wide-open attitude of the Signal Hill trials attracted the full spectrum of eccentrics. Longshoremen rode two-by-fours down the chute. Engineers from nearby military industrial think tanks campaigned such black-box exotics as air bearings and programmable down-force composite foils. Powers of the skate industry backed their quickest jocks. A miasma of fame and misfortune haunted all, and players broke out their most potent trick bags as they hunted it.

The 1977 Championships opened in a substantial rainstorm, and a number of riders lobbied for a postponement due to the unsafe conditions. O'Mahoney eyeballed the petitioners and said nothing, grabbing a bystander's board and shooting the hill himself.

Clockwise from top left: John Hutson discusses speed strategies from atop Signal Hill's staging area, June 1978; Henry Hester's White Lightning blows past a hillside of onlookers, June 1978; Ermico's legendary Stroker skate car.

Eventually bowing to consensus opinion (or, some said, sanity), O'Mahoney announced a delay date and invited the drenched competitors to his nearby nightclub, the Nut House. This three-story den of iniquity was on Sixth in Pedro, and Jim kept it operating 24 hours a day. O'Mahoney's headquarters had such amenities as a tournament billiards parlor, a shooting gallery, the first karaoke stage in the country, two full bars, a bandstand, and a three-bedroom apartment. Several racers took advantage of this "training" opportunity and stayed on for weeks.

The '77 edition of the speed soirée marked the genesis of Independent. "Smiley" Mike Goldman was competing in the thick of it for NHS/Santa Cruz/OJ, using conventional equipment. By far the weirdest competitor—and that is quite a statement in this context—was Terry Nails, who was shoehorned into an evil, sleek aluminum coffin put together by a bunch of upstarts from an unknown San Francisco entity called Ermico. The Harley-Davidson Racing Team attire worn by members of their pit crew alluded to their diabolical mechanical chops. Nails was a professional musician who was playing at the time in a band called Tommy Tutone. The displaced punk struggled in this bar band that eventually charted big with the pop ditty "Jenny Jenny." He didn't fit in onstage, and he was terrifically out of place here. Terry's ashen countenance made clear that the ghoul did not waste much of his life in daylight. But he ran quick during the deluge, and people paid attention to the sprung-strutted, steerable Stroker truck that he relied upon.

When the rescheduled contest finally went off, everyone was primed for mayhem. On hand was a brace of new skate cars that had obviously been inspired by the apparent speed of the Nails-driven Stroker-Ermico unit during the rained-out prelims. The resultant contest rescheduling had boosted the mixture of testosterone—and, in some cases, chemical enhancement—into a sanguine alchemy that reeked of disaster, speed, and big thrills. The extended ramp-up time over-amped many.

The bacchanalia of Signal Hill and O'Mahoney's neverending hospitality tend to preclude my complete recollection of these happenings. I can testify with certainty, though, that the Formula One–esque Stroker trucks broke ground and, by virtue of their complicated geometry and intricate structure, remain arguably the most advanced units ever. The other indelible impression that still hangs from the Hill finals is of Terry Nails driving his gravity-powered vehicle all the way through both sets of the hay-bale retaining barriers and out onto Redondo Boulevard, where he was run over by a car. I think Nails' best mark was just about 60 miles per hour, which put him way out in front of the competition and secured him a second-place finish. Henry Hester ran his Ermico-built Stroker car to a world-record-setting first place.

Epilogue: Signal Hill. There was one final grand downhill there, sponsored by O'Mahoney and the United States Skateboard Association in '78. Grand bonhomie and competitive attitude alike were obliterated when racer Tina Treffeton collided with a metal pole at speed. Her horrifying impact accentuated the underlying peril of the Signal Hill test. Everyone knew it was a situation fraught with danger that they had all signed on for willingly. On that day, 12 riders were seriously injured on the Hill.

NHS/Ermico/Independent-equipped test pilots like John Hutson, Mike Goldman, Bob Skoldberg, Cliff Coleman, and Jamie Hart were profoundly in evidence, taking the top five places in the stand-up class. Hutson broke the world record in the stand-up class on Indy 109s. Hester's White Lightning Stroker-Ermico skate car flew to second.

A topside view from the crest of Signal Hill's steep and short plunge. Note the hazardous intersecting train tracks at the bottom, June 1978.

"If you want to be safe, use double rubbers. If you want to skate, push off. If you don't want to skate, go home."

—James O'Mahoney

AHEAD
STOP

NHS and Ermico, two separate groups of Northern California outsiders, had come down to SoCal skate establishment Mecca and laid waste to everything sacred. Up until this instant, everything had been centered in Califas Del Sur, and quite frankly, the few who controlled things liked it that way. The pretenders were glum, as the more astute among them correctly realized that their money train had just been derailed.

Shuirman and Novak seized the moment and arranged an immediate parlay with Swenson and Vitello. A new confederation was forged and rapidly brought about an exotic suspension truck called Independent, which was essentially unbeatable in slalom from that point on.

An unsure thing beats a sure thing every time. Searching for feedback and not willing to content themselves with creating the unbeatable slalom unit, the coalition forces kept testing. Deconstructionist Rick Blackhart test-rode the archetype-setting slalom trucks and had the courage to point out the unthinkable: the super-successful independent suspension unit bogged down on the transitions of pool skating and did not offer enough resistance for vertical riding. Dr. Rick's prognosis flew in the face of prevailing wisdom. At that time, slalom was getting most of the mass-media exposure, and the industry felt that supporting timed racing events was the best way to promote the growth of the sport. Slalom was considered to be controllable, transportable, legal, and definitively athletic.

NHS had the strongest and most victorious slalom team there was, along with pro bowl ace Steve Olson. Blackhart was renowned for being a purveyor of trouble—he was adept at illegal pool sessioning, had herb that killed, liked trespassing on federal lands to skate giant pipes, and was a foul-mouthed and relentless political provocateur. Ricky was a spirit of the future who ecstatically tortured the ghosts of the past. Swenson and Vitello decided to endorse the creation of a fixed-axle truck that was true to Blackhart's dictates that "it's got to turn, and it shouldn't hang up." Shuirman and Novak added their backing to this latest round of pressure cooking. A week of 20-hour days of continual development passed, and Rick, Kevin Thatcher, and Steve Olson began trickling out prototype samples of what would prove to be the most successful geometry going.

Strong contest showings at Newark and the Big O honed it. Olson went on to win the overall world title and Skateboarder magazine's coveted Skateboarder of the Year award. By then the inmates were running the game, and the asylum was filled with former contenders who cried amongst themselves about passed glory.

Vitello worked the scene scouting talent. Stealing other companies' team riders? It was really more about finding those like-minded individuals who grasped the vision of what was possible with the 88s and 109s. I recall bringing an early set of 109s to a session where a big-time manufacturer and his top gun were present. The manufacturer always presented himself as a thoroughly professional engineer. He looked at my setup and soberly imparted, "These trucks will never work," and then ran out a bunch of garbage rhetorical equations about stability, polar moments of inertia, and dynamic loading. His celebrity endorsement rider tried my board, fell right to the ground, and looked very surprised that he couldn't ride it. Right then I realized that the Independent cartel had a big edge. Old was out and new was in—it was time to turn.

Exploring the Headwaters of Skate Creation

By C.R. Stecyk III

The Californication of the American Dream began at the precise moment when the western spirit of Manifest Destiny collided implacably with the infinite serenity and expanse of the Pacific Ocean. Social theorists continue to investigate this odd fusion of cultures, attitudes, and methodologies.

United States Route 66 was built in 1927. The largest human migration in American history occurred on this road, which wound more than 2,000 miles from Chicago, Illinois to Santa Monica, California. By 1932, politicians bragged that 66 was paved the entire length of the roadway. John Steinbeck dubbed it the "Mother Road." Will Rogers called it the "Main Street of America." All of the factors indispensable to widespread change had been set in motion. The population, cultural, and economic centers of the nation shifted to Cali.

At the end of the trail in Santa Monica Bay, guys like Tom Blake, Thomas Rogers, Myers Butte, Pete Petersen, Bob Simmons, Gardner Chapin, Joe Quigg, Dave Sweet, and Matt Kivlin combined modern materials from aircraft, house, and boat construction with the ancient art of surf riding, laying the foundations for current surfboard building. It was only a matter of time until one of them found all that cement just waiting to be ridden. The result: sidewalk surfing.

Let's get one piece of folkloric fiction out of the way: everybody's Uncle Albert knocked the wooden fruit crate off his two-by-four skate scooter on some long-forgotten blustery afternoon early in the last century. The tales are invariably the same, although the locations differ: the Bowery, Atlanta, Newport Beach, Boston, San Antonio, Seattle, the District of Columbia, and so forth. Many, if not most, of these stories are probably as true as they are archetypal.

For a time in the early '60s, all of the progressive surfers skated: Skip Frye, Butch Van Artsdalen, David Nuuhiwa, Mike Hynson, Herbie Fletcher, Mike Purpus, Joey Cabell, Gary Propper, John Severson, Mickey Muñoz, Lance Carson … the list goes on and on. Today, surfers on the pulse perform maneuvers pioneered by skaters. But motivated agents of change preceded surf media, business, and popular "I wanna be a beach boy boarding on the briny deep" hysteria. Just who "Adam" is for this new age is a matter of conjecture, but strong anecdotal evidence does provide some powerful clues about skating's primal origins. Keep in mind that surf riders are a tightly knit clan, interrelated via both formal and informal alliances. In the quest for illumination, I will drop a few names and their connections to the subject at hand.

Above, left to right: Steve and Barrie Boehne opt for a tandem descent on a set of urethane wheels, October 1975; Waldo Autry defies gravity at an untainted Mt. Baldy pipe, February 1976.

Somewhere in the vicinity of the headwaters of skate creation, there was no man with a plan. Spontaneity was the norm circa 1946. Gardner Chapin was gluing up composite skins with Simmons on Riverside Drive. On the workshop floor, roughing out a kid board in the wood chips, was Chapin's young stepson, Miklos "Miki" Sandor Dora. Quigg was in an alley off Olympic, where he had Kivlin in reserve. Simmons joined Quigg, and they began building styrofoam-core, wood-skinned, glassed boards. Petersen was playing with fiberglass on the Municipal Pier. George Downing came over on a boat from Hawaii and knocked the nose off his redwood board when it hit the Malibu pier. Simmons glued it back on with catalyzed resin, which was then an ultra-exotic material. The interchange launched into overdrive. The coastal boys were in the islands, and vice versa. In the middle of the proceedings, three kids got their first serious boards, all built by Joe Quigg. Those three—Phil Edwards, Greg Noll, and Miki Dora—went on to become the most influential wave riders of the '60s.

Edwards ended up being labeled the world's greatest and had the first signature-model skateboard at the Makaha organization, generally considered the first commercial skate company and founded by Larry Stevenson (who later patented the kicktail skateboard). Its label featured a graphic of "Tiki" Mike Doyle, who was the Makaha skate team manager and won the 1969 world surf title. To escape from the broiler of his ensuing surf stardom, Doyle made runs to Santa Cruz, where he hung with Novak, Haut, and Shuirman—three henchmen from an imminent corporate apocalypse. Skipper Boy Engblom was a Makaha factory grunt who branded the Phil Edwards logo onto the production sticks.

Noll is credited for breaking the size barrier in surfing by riding the period's largest wall and building the biggest surf factory. Greg also made films and built skateboards. Multiple world title holder George Downing, along with Buffalo Kealauana, Ben Aipa, world champions Fred Hemmings and Jimmy Blears, and many other Hawaiian individualists, passed time near Noll's camp. All of them skated some. Aipa honed boards for Larry Bertelman and, briefly, with Jeff Ho in Santa Monica. Ho (out of the Dewey Weber/Robert Milner factories) teamed with Engblom (Makaha, Velzy, et al.), and they founded Zephyr with the surf/skate Z-Boys. One of the other Ho designers was Makaha champ Craig Wilson, who had a friend named Alden Kaiokakau who could flow a dozen 360s in a row at overhead Ala Moana. Kaiokakau was the first skater to ride the Stroker prototype trucks. When a urethane whiz from Rhode Island, Tony Roderick, arrived at the Solar Surfboards shop in Santa Cruz, he was met by Rich Novak's statement, "A dollar twenty-five each, or forget it." He left a set of precision-bearing proto wheels; Jay Shuirman had him on the phone within the hour. The resultant fluke served up the Road Rider franchise.

Then there was Miki "Da Cat" Dora, the man who denied anything and everything. Except that he kept riding skateboards—before they were in,

through their acceptance, and after they were out. Through several incarnations and a nickname that celebrated his uncanny balance and feline style, Da Cat rolled. When it was said that Miki was the best rider in the world, he replied, "I don't live there." At the Malibu Invitational contest, he gleefully threw away his trophy and hung a BA. At the height of his fame, he dove into perpetual circumnavigation of the globe. Forevermore, Dora was neither here nor there long enough to be contained or catalogued, or to explain why he wasn't somewhere else befitting his stature.

At the finale of Miklos Sandor Chapin Dora III's tenure, he recalled "screwing around on this wheeled apparatus that Quigg had improvised to move things." Was this the first intentional act of sidewalk surfing? Just a kid called Da Cat, mucking about on a device ghetto-engineered by Slow Joe out of Douglas Surplus Annex industrial roller casters and shipping-pallet oak, in an alley in Santa Monica, circa 1947? I asked Miki this question directly, and with the necessary solemnity attending a great man's dying declaration. His answer: "Do not tell anyone anything but this: first, last, none of that matters."

Institutions of record, such as *The New York Times, The Washington Post, The Los Angeles Times,* Prime Media, and AOL Time Warner, noted his passing. Not one mentioned that he was a skater.

Clockwise from top: *LA County's Vermont Drop was a notorious hotbed of skate activity where the masses dialed in tricks and earned their licks, May 1975; Dropping low pivotal turns, Tony Alva mystifies the crowd at the Del Mar Fairgrounds National Championships, April 1975; Jay Adams drops from a tabletop, Northridge, CA, June 1975.*

The Independent Revolution

By Bob Denike

The founders of Independent Truck Company are Fausto Vitello, Eric Swenson, Jay Shuirman, and Richard Novak. To know these four is to discover the essence of Independent: skateboarding, having fun, making money, improving products, a desire to win, and letting skaters be skaters—all with a "do it yourself/fuck off" attitude.

Fausto and Eric met in the U.S. Army Reserve in 1969, working in an engineering unit in Sausalito, just north of the Golden Gate Bridge in San Francisco. The mutual preoccupations they discovered while working together—wrenching on cars and motorcycles, loud music, partying, going fast, and trying to figure out how to go faster—designated them as "greasers." Fausto was thrown out of the Army after a vehicle in his charge mysteriously fell off a cliff and was completely destroyed. Soon after, Eric left on a medical discharge, the result of a severe motorcycle accident. It wasn't much of a stretch to find them, by 1974, wrenching for the Harley-Davidson motorcycle race team as crew mechanics and backing up racer Scott Brelsford at the AMA Professional National motorcycle racing series.

Their new vocation was ideal for sharpening their understanding of all things mechanical. And more important, it taught them to listen to and communicate with pro motorcycle racers, to tweak and improve the bikes, and dream of winning. John Solimine, another friend in the race circuit, recalls,

"We were hanging out with some serious people in research and development. We all lived in the pursuit of championships."

As the Harley deal dried up over time, Fausto and Eric slid over to help Erv Kanamoto, renowned crew chief for the Kawasaki race team. They got involved in R & D on a three-cylinder, two-stroke, flat-track motorcycle, an advantageous innovation that backroom politics ultimately banned; Harley-Davidson was instrumental in removing the multi-cylinder, two-stroke engine from the tour. This would not be the last time Fausto and Eric would develop advanced technologies that were perceived as "unfair."

When their work for Kanamoto ended, the two resorted to odd jobs to make ends meet. They would work just long enough to make a few bucks and then head to the beach or the bars in the evening. This routine all changed permanently, however, during a fateful meeting/party in the Haight-Ashbury district of San Francisco in 1976. Surf champ Alden Kaiokakau had flown over from Hawaii with his buddy, SF street hustler Michael Kelly. They got together at friend Michael Parry's house, where they met Fausto Vitello. During the ensuing bullshit session, Kelly tells Parry and Fausto, "Skateboarding is the next big thing."

Fausto was already mildly interested in skateboarding; Kelly's declaration was all he needed to hear. He and Eric bailed on their spotty employment and took the initial steps toward what would eventually become Ermico Enterprises Inc., a small machine shop on Yosemite Avenue in San Francisco. The company name Er-mic-o was derived from a combination of the partners' names: ERic, MIChael Parry (who later left the business), and FaustO.

Fausto and Eric complemented each other perfectly, with Fausto out front and Eric backing him up in the production arena. "Eric was to Fausto what 'Cast Iron Charlie' [Charlie Sorenson] was to Henry Ford," states Solimine. "Their exposure in major league professional racing uniquely equipped them to take skateboard development to the limit."

Solimine was soon brought in and asked to sketch some initial product concepts. Based on the first few rough drawings and ideas, Fausto went with a skateboard truck that had independent steering. In the machine shop of museum-exhibit designer Norman Weiss, near the Palace of Fine Arts in San Francisco, Solimine created the first "Stroker" truck proto-type. Solimine was instrumental in teaching Fausto and Eric about the various ins and outs of setting up a machine shop and the complexities of running a production facility.

Solimine remembers, "When two trucks were finished and mounted on a skateboard, Kelly picked up the board in SF, bought it a seat on an airplane, and flew back to give it to the surf champ to test. Kaiokakau rode it off curbs and walls, broke it, and asked for another. We cleaned up the design and immediately went into production."

The Ermico gang's next goal was to win the prestigious downhill race at Signal Hill in Long Beach, California in 1977. The NorCal guys came in with more of a motorcycle-gang vibe and shocked the laid-back SoCal surfer scene prevalent in skateboarding at the time. To say the least, they were not welcomed with open arms. With a Stroker on the front and a straight-axle truck on the back,

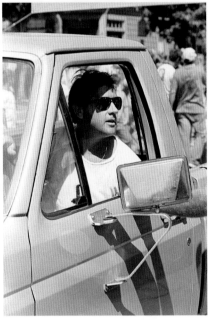

Clockwise from top left: *Independent Truck Company's gang of four: Novak, Vitello, Jay Shuirman (with Steve Olson), and Eric Swenson. They understood what was right for skateboarding and became so powerful that the industry insiders on the other side of the fence didn't stand a chance. Opposite page: Fausto Vitello and Rich Novak shake up the scene at Winchester Skatepark.*

SF hill bomber Terry Nails rode lying down in a lean-steering position inside a revolutionary Solimine-designed aluminum "skate car." He tripped the clock at just under 60 miles per hour and almost killed himself along the way. Ed Riggins, a friend of Fausto and Eric and part of the skate car race "crew," remembers, "When it was showtime, we were sent down past the finish line in case Nails couldn't stop the car. The hay bales were right behind us, and behind them was an intersection with heavy cross traffic. Down the hill he came, and we instantly knew he couldn't stop. He was real low and coming on like a missile. We tried to catch the car, but he flew by in a heartbeat and broke through the hay bales, narrowly missing the cross traffic and innocent bystanders." The next-fastest racer was clocked at 40 miles per hour. A rain delay postponed the event, and a few months later, many other racers showed up, chasing Nails and Ermico in skate cars of their own. Nails came in second, and Henry Hester came in first, utilizing the same Stroker truck and a similar skate car setup.

Aside from this major upset achievement, the Stroker truck was not a commercial success. But it did create a potential upside. John Politis, childhood friend of Eric and early Ermico employee, remembers, "The truck design may not have been accepted, but it did catch the eye of Richard Novak and Jay Shuirman." Jay and Rich, by then already entrenched in the skateboard business, were intrigued by the Stroker's steering mechanism, and, adds Politis, "They were working on their own truck design with independent suspension."

Jay and Richard first met when they were teenagers, in 1957; Rich was throwing dirt clods off a sea cliff at the group Jay was hanging with on the beach below. It was a classic confrontation between Santa Cruz surfers and jocks from the Valley. Ironically, a long-standing friendship bloomed from this initial confrontation/introduction. Together, Jay and Rich surfed, partied, traveled to Hawaii and Mexico, hassled kooks, and generally raised hell.

In 1963, Rich began working with Doug Haut, a close friend and local surfboard shaper, in various surfboard production shops around town. In their mid- to late twenties, Rich, Doug, and Jay started their own surfboard business, Solar Surfboards, driven by the idea that they would play as much as possible and work the shop only when the waves were not cooperating.

But by 1969, Jay was attending college and had started a family, and the three friends had to search for steady and legitimate work. They parlayed their surfboard manufacturing experience into distributing raw materials for surfboards, ultra-light sailboats, motorcycle fairings, and auto bodies. A new company called NHS (Novak, Haut, and Shuirman) was born in the back of their small shop on 41st Avenue in Santa Cruz.

Jimmy Phillips, a childhood friend of the pair, recalls their early success: "Jay and Rich had a habit of making phone calls with both of them on the line at the same time. It was impossible to say no to them, because when one stopped talking, the other would jump right in. I believe that's one reason they became so powerful: the businessmen on the other end of the line didn't stand a chance."

By 1973, skateboard hype was reaching a fever pitch. Through Jimmy Hoffmann, a childhood friend of Jay's living in Hawaii, NHS was asked by McKully Bike Shop on Oahu if they could locate a supplier of skateboards on the mainland. One thing quickly led to another, and NHS built 500 Santa Cruz skateboards, made of pultruded fiberglass and complete with Sure Grip trucks and Roller Sport loose ball-bearing wheels. When a reorder quickly came in for 500 more, Santa Cruz Skateboards was on the map.

Doug Haut chose to split from NHS to focus on shaping surfboards. Jay and Rich stayed on board, gleaning sales, distribution, and promotion knowledge from the dynamic skateboard industry. The Jay/Rich partnership was mutually beneficial. Tim Piumarta, an early Santa Cruz team rider, witnessed the pair at work: "Jay was the creative side of the Novak/Shuirman team," states Piumarta, "with Novak a bit more grounded on the business side … they were in perfect counterbalance."

As Jay and Rich began selling their skateboards locally and in other NorCal areas, they set up a small production line, hand-assembling the skateboards, trucks, and wheels. Jay, always in motion, knocked over a five-gallon drum of loose ball bearings one day, and more than 300,000 spilled out onto the wood floor. Looking down at the agonizing mess, the partners realized there had to be a better way.

Shortly thereafter, through sheer coincidence and luck, a manufacturer's rep named Tony Roderick entered the surf shop holding a urethane wheel; their lives would never be the same after that day.

Roderick worked for an East Coast urethane company selling commercial rollers for business machines. He had seen a *Surfer* magazine ad for skateboard wheels and had the revolutionary idea of combining precision bearings used for copy-machine rollers with a urethane wheel. He left a set of his wheels at the shop for Jay and Rich to test. By the time Roderick had returned to his house across town, Jay had left six animated phone messages. The first-ever precision-bearing wheels, Road Rider Wheels, were born that day. By 1976, the NHS boys and Roderick had created a powerhouse, selling and distributing over six million wheels throughout an unbeatable worldwide network.

Jay and Rich were united by their shared desire to affiliate themselves with winners and to constantly innovate. They improved NHS' Road Rider, OJ, and Park Rider Wheels consistently, basing their modifications on feedback from top skateboarding pros, and they enjoyed an almost-uncontested run through 1977. NHS also introduced the first commercially available laminated-maple skateboard deck, the 5-Ply, which Steve Olson rode en route to winning the 1978 Hester Pro Bowl series. NHS also dominated the slalom-racing circuit with John Hutson, Henry Hester, and the SC Graphite Loaded slalom board.

With a firm hold on the deck and wheel business, Jay and Rich set their sights on skateboard trucks and began initial-concept

Randall Buck experiments with a set of suspension trucks in Newark's keyhole pool while Novak, Vitello, Tim Piumarta, and Swenson check the action, May 1978.

R & D on a truck with full independent suspension. The pair initially attended the Signal Hill race, hoping to dominate this speed contest with their urethane formulas and thereby boast the fastest wheel in skateboarding. At the '77 Signal Hill race, Mike Goldman took top honors riding OJ Wheels, standing up and clocking 50 miles per hour. At the '78 race, after a year of intense R & D work, Park Rider Wheels and Independent Trucks swept the top three spots in the stand-up division, with John Hutson, Mike Goldman, and Bob Skoldberg taking first, second, and third, respectively.

The Ermico crew's powerful presence at Signal Hill impressed Jay and Rich; likewise, Fausto and Eric were intrigued by NHS' success. With their roots in the then-less-respected NorCal region, they naturally gravitated toward each other. NHS asked Ermico to fine-tune a design for the suspension truck; the essential premise of the deal was, "You make it, and we'll sell it." At the time, Ermico had introduced another truck, the Rebound; NHS distributed it for a short period, but it proved to be too unconventional.

NHS' various attempts at a suspension truck resulted in a torsion bar/rocker arm system. Conceptually effective, it suffered from two drawbacks: the torsion-bar suspension components were not yet fully functional, and the truck itself, which carried the suspension apparatus, was not fully developed. With input from various team riders, including Steve Olson (NHS' test pilot) and Rick Blackhart (Ermico's choice), they arrived at the simple concept of extracting the best features from two trucks on the market and combining and improving them to form a hybrid design.

Steve Olson's "Who's Hot" bio, in the April 1978 issue of *Skateboarder* magazine leaked the news of this development. Olson stated that the truck design would provide "the turning of a Bennett—but you can tighten it down like a Tracker." Ermico conceived the conventional truck design, and NHS added its concepts for the suspension components, utilizing the torsion bar/rocker arm system. The Independent Suspension Truck was born. The design dominated the racing scene and quickly became the most winning truck in slalom. When further tests proved that the suspension system would not work in bowls, the founders also introduced a straight-axle truck.

With this truck design in hand, the founders set their sights on the Hester Pro Bowl contest in Newark, NorCal and simply took the place by storm. D. David Morin, a rep for Kryptonic Wheels, recalls this event: "Independent hit the scene more like a Formula One race team invasion than some little skate company. The skaters were tough and anti-everything; they blew everyone away with attitude and let their skating do the talking. Sure, the product was great, but the sizzle was greater than the steak."

The final result at Newark: four of the top eight winners rode Independent trucks, including first place, Bobby Valdez, and second place, Rick Blackhart.

Independent capped its dominance in 1978, when the top five point-total finalists in the completed Hester Series rode Independent Trucks. In less than a year, all the top riders were signing on with Independent.

As 1978 came to a close, Independent was on its way. The Gang of Four was hungry for victory, and the ingredients were all there: Jay and Rich had the established connections and distribution, and Fausto and Eric could provide the development and production necessary to complete a superior equation. Out of serendipitous events, raw talent, and a common purpose emerged a better skateboard truck and a brand that would become a revolution and forever redefine skateboarding.

"Surf more and work less. Always party at work and work a party." —Jay Shuirman

Clockwise from top left: *Vitello hustles a collection of essential gems; Swenson usually put in time behind serious tools; Vitello gets tubed at SF's famed EMB, December 1980; NHS founders, Novak, Shuirman, and Doug Haut; portrait of Shuirman; Novak on board; Shuirman provides comic relief; Terry Nails and Vitello wait out the rain at Signal Hill, June 1977.*

public enemy
NUMBER ONE ✠✠✠✠ By Fausto Vitello

I want to set the record straight: there would be no Independents without Rick Blackhart. He was the man who set Eric and me on the right course to build the best skateboard truck. I met Rick and his cohort Kevin Thatcher in Santa Cruz on a day when he was harassing the NHS crew at their old 41st Avenue headquarters. Rick was not a man of many words, but as far as he was concerned, just about everything being made for skateboarding in those days was fucked. His board was an add-on kicktail, custom made by KT; the wheels were hard-ass Tunnel Rocks, and the trucks were Trackers. He had a hand in designing the board and wheels, so he was cool with that. The trucks, on the other hand, were unacceptable: they didn't turn, they hung up, and they didn't grind right. We were working on a suspension truck with Jay Shuirman and Novak, so I approached Blackhart about helping us design it. In typical Rick fashion, he gave me this "Who in the fuck are you?" attitude. I tried several times to get him to respond, but I got nowhere. In his mind, the whole Santa Cruz scene was a complete loss: he was a pool skater from San Jose, and they were wimpy slalom riders from the beach.

Eric and I were essentially broke. We had already tried to get into the market twice with projects that had failed, and we didn't have enough money to do another. We had made a few sets of Independent Suspension Trucks for Jay and Novak, and they had paid us well; I think they had given us about four grand for six or eight trucks. They had been fucking around with the suspension idea for years but had never made it work. We made the concept succeed by coming up with what was basically a torsion bar arrangement. Problem was, after about a day of riding them, the trucks tended to get sprung and had to be rebuilt. They worked great for slalom, and Bulky Olson kind of liked them in pools and banked slalom, but Bulky could ride anything, and equipment was the least of his concerns. Blackhart thought the whole deal was a joke, but we couldn't get to him to talk to us about how he would improve it.

Eric and I liked Rick from the get-go; he had a two-door '61 Ford with the best sound system he could afford and a rolling skateboard shop in the trunk. His main music was hard rock, and Ted Nugent was his man. He was

definitely our kind of guy, and what finally ended our stalemate was our common interest in "brewskys and reefer." Once we got that part together, communication with The Doctor was no problem.

Rick's mandate was simple: to make a better truck, you didn't have to reinvent the "Chicago pivot." What you did need to do was make it turn, make it grind, make it lightweight, and prevent it from hanging up (pre-ollie). We already had a model that we had designed for the suspension truck; by removing the torsion bar and sticking an axle in it, it became a standard truck. We had some castings made and added the axle, and we had our truck. I called Rick and made an appointment to meet with him in San Jose, but Rick didn't trust anyone, including Eric and me. He'd been burned so many times by industry types that he didn't want to be a partner; all he wanted was cash and brews. I tried to talk him into a partnership, 'cause money was limited, but he demanded 200 bucks and a case of Heinies as compensation.

We scrapped the money together and headed down to San Jose. Rick still thought the whole deal was a scam, so he wanted his payment before he would do anything. Once the deal was done, he had to drive around and get KT, and then we had to assemble a board. KT made the boards, and all he had that day was one that wasn't quite right, so we had to talk Rick into riding it. The whole thing took hours, but we finally had the board together and were ready to test. Rick jumped on his board reluctantly and rode across the parking lot. He did some gyrating and smacked the board (truck first) against a parking block. He rode across again, lifted the nose, and smacked the rear truck against the parking block. He did this a couple more times and then rode toward us. Just as he was about to shank me in the shins, he lifted the nose, did a 90-degree turn, and came to a stop. He flipped the board and said, "These things are all right, but they need to turn more and hang up less." He explained how the rear hoop of the hanger was hitting before the wheels and how "that sucked." That was it. Because they didn't work right, he couldn't be bothered to ride them anymore. We hung around the parking lot and torched a few and drank some brews. We got to know each other a little more and promised to return with all the changes he wanted. As always, he was still skeptical. No matter how much you smoked and drank with him, he still felt like you were out to burn him.

We shot back up to San Francisco, and the next day, Eric welded up the trucks and made the necessary changes to tuck the yoke and change the geometry so the trucks would turn more. We called Rick and told him we were ready to test again. He couldn't believe that we had done a new truck overnight. It was back to San Jose with 200 bucks and a case of Heinies, but this time I brought some bush to sweeten the deal. When we got there, we had to go through the same shit, with Rick and KT disagreeing about everything. We finally got it together, and off he went across the parking lot. This time, the routine produced different results and a clear statement. While downing a brew and taking a big puff, Rick said, "If you make these trucks, everyone will ride them." Eric and I couldn't believe it. It was the first positive statement to come out of Rick's mouth. He rode the trucks a few more times, and every time he was stoked. He wanted to keep

Rick's first ad, he wanted the word "fucking" in there. But there was no way that *Skateboarder* magazine, which was a Christian company, would allow swearing of any kind. We had to settle for "#★X⚡!!!" instead; as it turned out, it was better than "fucking," and we've used it ever since.

I'm not an artist or photographer, and I had never done an advertising campaign. But I did have a lot of ideas, and I was fortunate enough to meet a guy who showed me the way and became my best friend. The guy's name was Craig Stecyk. At that time, he worked for *Skateboarder*. He had written some of the most memorable pieces in that mag, and he also wrote "Off the Wall" every month. He was like the prophet of skateboarding. We would talk for hours about skateboarding, cars, machinery, motorcycles, art, and everything in between. We would see each other at contests and always hung out together. He taught me about photography and about how to do an ad campaign. To him, skateboarding was, and is, artistic self-expression. He created some of Independent's most memorable ads and

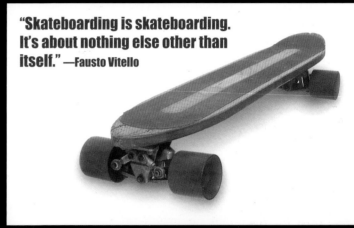

"Skateboarding is skateboarding. It's about nothing else other than itself." —Fausto Vitello

them, but we needed them to make the patterns to produce the trucks. A few more brews and smokes settled the issue, and we took the trucks with the promise to return and ride a better set in a pool. Jay Shuirman showed up while we were hanging around and was surprised that we had Rick testing the trucks. It was incredible; we were going to do this deal, and it was based on Rick's knowledge and our common love of smoking and drinking.

The next day in San Francisco, we went to see an old pattern maker on Bryant Street and had him create the patterns for the trucks. We left there and went to Santa Cruz to discuss the deal with Jay and Novak. We had no money. What we did have was a truck and a desire to make money so we could do some serious partying. We been working on the independent suspension truck, and we all liked the name Independent. Then Jay said, "All kids want to be independent," and that was it. It was Independent Truck Company from then on. Jay had a *Time* magazine with a picture of the Pope in it, and he said we should make the iron cross on his crown the Independent logo. It all came together just like that, and then we went out to have dinner and made our deal. A couple days later, we went to a restaurant and signed the deal. It was really easy, and it still stands to this day.

While the tooling was underway, we had some one-off castings made and flowed the trucks to Rick, KT, and Olson. We also made a few more suspension trucks for the slalom riders to use. It was like a revolution; skateboarding was taking its cyclical shit, and we were coming out with a truck that everyone craved. Jay ordered a quarter of a million Independent stickers and made a bunch of T-shirts. The guys decided I should be the front man, and they cut me loose to do whatever I wanted. Everyone had a role, and it seemed pretty easy, especially for me. I just figured I would go out, travel, and rage. I liked all the guys we had been working with, especially Rick, Olson, and KT. We were all in it for the same reason: to have a good time.

Someone had to do the ads, and Rick, who always tried to push the envelope, wanted the image to be hard. In those days, the hard shit was Alva and Dogtown; the rest were pretty much surf-oriented companies that were doing skateboarding because there was a buck to be made. For

wrote the motto that is the essence of Independent: "Built to Grind." That motto and that one ad with the nude chick with the Indy stickers on her nipples were what set *TWS* in motion. They were about Skate and Create; we were about Skate and *Destroy*.

Over the years, one person has always supported my endeavors, and that's my wife, Gwynn. Early on, when we were trying to start our company, she hit the road with me and helped promote Independent and skateboarding. Skaters stayed at my house, and to them, she was one of us, so to me, she's part of Independent.

Many skaters have come and gone in the near-30 years that Indy has been around. Some—like Blackhart, Olson, and KT—are the cornerstone of the company. Others—like Bobby Valdez (who won the first contest on Indys), Steve and Micke Alba, Duane Peters, Steve Caballero, Brad Bowman, Lance Mountain, James Muir, Billy Ruff, David Z, Rodney Mullen, John Hutson, Henry Hester, Bob Skoldberg, Jerry "Taters" Hurtado, Peter Gifford, Scott Foss, Eric Dressen, Scott Oster, Bug Martino, Rick Howard, Tommy Guerrero, Julien Stranger, John Cardiel, Gonz, Danny Way, Jake Nunn, Danny Sargent, and Tony Trujillo—have all contributed to the legend. The riders who have bought Indys have also become part of the family. It's the step you take to become legit.

Of course, we've also lost some people to the great park in the sky or the furnace below, and no loss is greater than Jay Shuirman. Jay was one of the coolest guys I ever had the pleasure of knowing. He was a hard-ass partier and businessman; he could get in your face one minute and be partying with you the next. He was great at putting shit together and letting you do what you liked. Fuck, he would join in anytime to have fun. His specialty was burning on his partner, Novak. Not long after the launch of Indys, he succumbed to a serious illness and passed on. What he left behind was a philosophy of letting skaters be skaters. I'll forever miss him.

Throughout the history of Independent, I have always tried to maintain the "fuck off" attitude of the company founders. I've never had my partners tell me who to have on a team or how to do the ads; it's always been easy, and it's always been about skateboarding.

we wrote our
OWN RULES ✠ ✠ ✠ ✠ By Richard Novak

At the 1975 Cadillac Bahne Skateboard contest in L.A., three things changed skateboarding and established it as an industry, not a fad. A crazy eccentric named Ron Bennett introduced the Bennett truck, designed specifically for skateboarding. Dave McIntyre was there with the G & S Fiberflex skateboard. And Jay Shuirman, Tony Roderick, and I had the first precision-bearing skateboard wheel: the Road Rider.

These three products arrived in the business at around the same time, set the high-water mark for performance, and created the foundation for what we know now as the skateboard industry. Around that same time, Jay and I and a few others in this group developed the standard skateboarding formula: we set the profit margins for the industry, which initially established the profits necessary to run a proper business and reinvest in marketing, teams, and product innovation.

By '77, slalom racing was the showpiece of skateboarding, and Jay and I attacked it with a vengeance. We wanted the best products on the best riders, and we wanted to win. With R & D help from Bob Willis at Quality Products/Road Rider, we had the capacity to take any wheel idea or urethane formula imaginable and make it a reality. Jay and I had backgrounds in composite materials, so we were always fooling around with board design. We soon had the best wheels and graphite loaded boards, but we still wanted an extra edge that would be inaccessible to our competitors. Ron Bennett was not too workable (to put it mildly), so we had a void in truck design. We were selling quite a few Trackers at the time, but we needed our own truck to distribute and wanted to develop a better skateboard-specific truck for racing.

Our first instinct was to look at how cars worked, as they had independent suspension that afforded wheels full contact with the surface. Jay and I would lie under glass tables and have John Hutson and Tim Piumarta turn a skateboard so we could see how much wheel would hit the surface. We fooled around with many ideas, made some castings, welded up some trucks, and finally came up with the concept of the torsion-bar system. The idea was to have it for different weights so you could replace worn-out torsion bars without replacing the whole truck. We

were designing higher-rebound, harder wheels, and this truck allowed for designing narrower, more tire-like wheels that rolled faster. We had a working design that we could retrofit current trucks with, but we soon ran into a major problem: we couldn't get the quantities we needed with consistent quality.

About this time, we met Eric, Fausto, and John Solimine, who were at some of the races with their Stroker Truck. A short while after, they also came out with a double-cushion truck, the Rebound, and we cut a deal: if we distributed the Rebound for them, they would develop and produce the suspension truck. Those poor riders we had on the Rebound … it worked, but it would have sudden lapses. Tim Piumarta broke both wrists at one time on that truck.

Fausto and Eric started to come to Santa Cruz and discuss truck design with Jay and me. One day Rick Blackhart was hanging around at NHS, and Jay asked him to talk to Fausto and Eric about the truck we were working on. Fausto and Eric were pretty raw and broke at the time, but they were eager to have a hit in the skateboard truck business. We were all sitting in the NHS office; Jay had a Tracker in one hand and a Bennett in another, and he handed them to Fausto and said, "Make a truck that turns like a Bennett and wears like a Tracker."

We tested the first design for the new truck with John Hutson, Tim Piumarta, and Steve Olson. Getting the design dialed eventually required that Jay and Olson tinker with the truck at the skateparks and that Rick Blackhart working directly with Fausto and Eric as their test rider. These efforts resulted in the Independent truck design. Although the suspension truck was exactly what we wanted for racing, it was expensive to make and had a limited market, so we soon moved to a straight-axle design.

With this new truck, we were on our way. It was exactly what skateboarding was waiting for, and it made great skaters ride even better. Independent just took off, with the four of us working hard to take over the truck business. Toward the end of the '70s, we realized that the people we were dealing with and competing against had no foresight for the skateboard business. The "leaders" at the time either had somebody fronting for them or were looking to the toy companies to buy them out so they could bank it and move to paradise. No one was in it for the long term except us.

In 1978, *Skateboarder* magazine was the leading trade publication; skaters who wanted coverage in it had to pray to the publisher and then bribe the editor. With a gram of Peruvian marching dust and a free surfboard, you might get your picture on the cover. Or, if you were a certain Santa Barbara company at the time, you would wait until everybody else had turned in their *Skateboarder* ads, visit the mag personally to check out the competing merchandise, and then produce your own ad.

The magazine officially denied it could happen, just as I watched the Wonder Boy from Santa Barbara put his back-cover ad together at the storyboard. It was all bullshit; they were so lame that they even blackballed Tony Alva and Steve Olson from the magazine for being "too punk." I'm sure they felt pretty stupid when Alva and Olson won their fucking skater poll shortly thereafter. *Skateboarder* magazine was so cool and brilliant

By spearheading *Thrasher* magazine and promoting downhill, street style, and backyard ramp events, Fausto laid the foundation for others to follow or completely deny, and we supported him as much as possible. I know skateboarding would not be where it is today without Fausto's work in the early '80s.

Collectively, we didn't give a rat's ass about anybody in the skateboard truck business. Tracker had gotten rid of Dave Dominy, the only creative and devoted truck person other than us, and that left nobody to further innovate trucks. We accomplished the same thing with Indy that we had with Road Rider and Park Rider: getting the best team we could find on the best products we could make.

It just exploded into the biggest surge the industry had ever seen, with the proper margins necessary to sustain promotion, riders, demos, R & D, and contests. It made the industry fun, and, unlike in the surf industry, the hard-goods manufacturers controlled the skate business.

 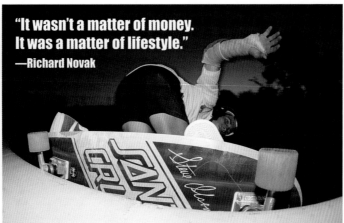 

that they eventually decided to become *Action Now,* a magazine that was soon gone.

By 1979 and into 1980, a bust hit the skate industry, and the market collapsed, just as vert bowl skating was taking hold. For me, it was a double hit: NHS' revenue declined sharply, and Jay, my best friend and business partner, died. It was a huge setback for me. Jay was Independent Trucks; he established the ads, the team, and the marketing, and he was meticulous about every detail. This all landed in my lap.

Fortunately, Jay and I had spent a lot of time with Fausto and Eric, and they quickly picked up the things we had learned over the years. They both stepped up big time, and we all decided that Fausto would take over the marketing and team, Eric would run production, and I would finance and distribute. Eric worked his ass off making trucks, and I kept things moving with my customer contacts around the world. But Fausto had the toughest job of all: he not only kept Independent going with the team and image but also resurrected the skateboard industry from its lowest point.

After *Skateboarder/Action Now* went out of business, Fausto, Eric, and I started *Thrasher* magazine in 1981. We knew nothing about the magazine biz, but Fausto took it upon himself to learn, and we asked that he do it quickly because we had very little time and no money. To be as fair as we could, we decided to give all the other skateboard companies first choice on ad page placement. Wonder Boy was the only one to choose the back cover; the rest were waiting for the second coming of Christ or something. We quickly enjoyed insane growth, so we could do what we wanted, and we wrote our own rules.

After racing was dead, we picked up the best vert and pool skaters and the people with the most radical "I don't give a fuck" attitude. We even cherry-picked the Ozzy and Harriet team from Santa Barbara with Stacy and Stecyk's help. The first punk ad, which showed Olson doing a low street move, was the last ad prepared by Jay Shuirman, and the entire venture was a major departure from the image that *Skateboarder* was trying to push.

This industry boom ended in the late '80s and early '90s, but Independent was still at the top. Ex-freestyle skateboarder Steve Rocco shook up the industry, taking on Powell and Vision by splitting from Santa Monica Airlines and eventually forming World Industries. It was the greatest marketing move since we had blown apart the wheel market with Speed Wheels. Rocco pretty much put Powell to bed; facing the same fate that had befallen the surf industry for the past 40 years, Powell then had to throw away the margin formula and wipe out 25 years of good margins for lower prices. But we adapted as others stuck their heads in the sand.

Despite all this upheaval, Indy has always remained on top because we don't give a fuck about anybody else except the Indy riders and customers. We've always run it like we did on day one; Fausto still has daily contact with the team and ads, and Eric and I still talk weekly to set production. Changes come from the team through Joey Tershay, and then we all do our best to execute. We've never changed the truck just for the sake of change, only to better it, and we all still live by this rule. I see so many companies change, change, change, thinking that it is going to increase sales—but when they have a shitty product to begin with, it doesn't matter how much they change.

We all had one main thing in common: we were driven to make better products, and we were never satisfied with what was on the market, or even with what we were making at the time; we always knew it could be better. We were determined to innovate, to listen to the riders and give them what they wanted. Innovation was always the core of NHS; it was what Jay and I believed in, and it spilled over into Independent Trucks.

From left: *Novak poised for success, 1977; Skateboarding was due for a big change following the Hester Series' first professional bowl contest, Spring Valley, CA, March 18, 1978; Inside NHS' production area, Santa Cruz 5-ply decks get screenprinted for the masses, 1977; Steve Olson lets loose on a pair of Stage I trucks at Winchester, August 1978; Olson takes a break from a truck testing session at Newark's brand-spanking-new keyhole, May 1978.*

origin of a SPECIES

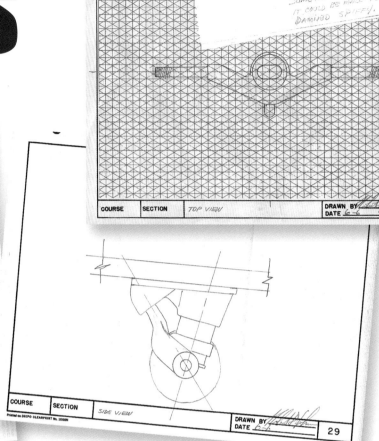

June 6

JAY,
      On the plane ride home Monday I had time to reflect on all that was said pertaining to truck geometry and the current rider feedback that has resulted in your present design of the solid axle indy truck.
      It seems certain, from both rider info and the performance of our in- dependent suspension truck, that the correct axle disposition lies in a plane parallel to the center line of the cushion king pin bolt.
      Your present design approaches that "ideal" location, however by utilis- ing a full width, one piece axle, it is impossible to properly locate it directly over the king pin bolt due to obvious interference problems.
      What I propose is the enclosed configuration, that would utilise all of the low profile geometry (angles etc.) of the current indy solid axle truck but would also include the most important parameter of correct axle location, which appears to be the key to truck stability and proper turning performance. This design would also satisfy the present rider preferences i.e., truck stiffness and no "loss of energy".
      I also propose that the axle yoke be investment cast in one piece from 17‑4 PH material (stainless) with no machining involved with the exception of 5/16‑24 axle threads, and from what I learned at P.F.I. this cluld surely be done in the $4.00 range and even less in quantitys in excess of 1500 piece batches.
      You have to admit it does have certain cosmetic appeal, especially being made from stainless and then tumbled to a shiny finish.
      Needless to say, if you found this idea marketable, a 2% kickback would not be too outlandish.

                                                — Bob

JAY: THE DRAWING, AS PRESENTED, UNDOUBTEDLY IS FAR TOO BEEFY AND COULD BE THINNED DOWN CONSIDERABLY WITH PROPER GUSSETING, FURTHER LOWERING THE COST OF THE CASTING.

• Hand-drafted hanger concepts illustrating an offset axle, aligned with the kingpin.

• A side view of the offset axle concept, demonstrating further how the axle and wheel line up with the kingpin.

• This letter illustrates communications regarding truck geometry and the advantages of an offset axle truck.

• These hand-welded truck prototypes show crude torsion bars controlling the movement of the rocker arms, allowing each axle to move independently.

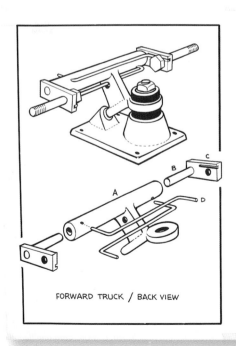

FORWARD TRUCK / BACK VIEW

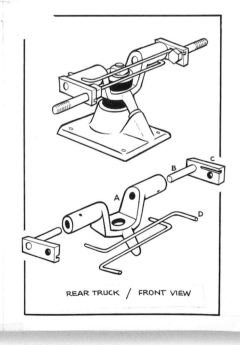

REAR TRUCK / FRONT VIEW

• Early suspension drawings show Jay Shuirman's vision of a rocker arm suspension concept. Note the different configurations for the front and back trucks.

• This group of working prototypes evidences many attempts to discover a revolutionary new truck design.

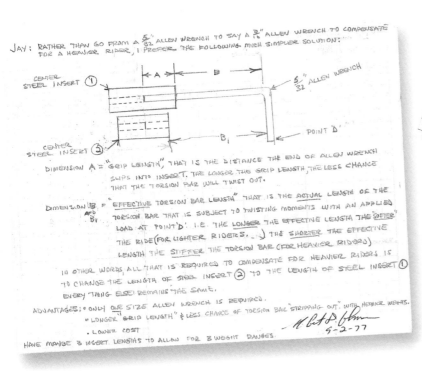

JAY: RATHER THAN GO FROM A 5/32" ALLEN WRENCH TO SAY A 1/8" ALLEN WRENCH TO COMPENSATE FOR A HEAVIER RIDER, I PREFER THE FOLLOWING MUCH SIMPLER SOLUTION:

CENTER STEEL INSERT ①

CENTER STEEL INSERT ②

5/32" ALLEN WRENCH

POINT 'D'

DIMENSION A = "GRIP LENGTH", THAT IS THE DISTANCE THE END OF ALLEN WRENCH SLIPS INTO INSERT. THE LONGER THE GRIP LENGTH, THE LESS CHANCE THAT THE TORSION BAR WILL TWIST OUT.

DIMENSION B AND B₁ = "EFFECTIVE TORSION BAR LENGTH" THAT IS THE ACTUAL LENGTH OF THE TORSION BAR THAT IS SUBJECT TO TWISTING MOMENTS WITH AN APPLIED LOAD AT POINT 'D'. I.E. THE LONGER THE EFFECTIVE LENGTH THE "SOFTER" THE RIDE (FOR LIGHTER RIDERS,) THE SHORTER THE EFFECTIVE LENGTH THE STIFFER THE TORSION BAR (FOR HEAVIER RIDERS)

IN OTHER WORDS, ALL THAT IS REQUIRED TO COMPENSATE FOR HEAVIER RIDERS IS TO CHANGE THE LENGTH OF STEEL INSERT ② TO THE LENGTH OF STEEL INSERT ① EVERY THING ELSE REMAINS THE SAME.

ADVANTAGES: • ONLY ONE SIZE ALLEN WRENCH IS REQUIRED.
• "LONGER GRIP LENGTH" & LESS CHANCE OF TORSION BAR "STRIPPING OUT" WITH HEAVIER WEIGHTS.
• LOWER COST

HAVE MAYBE 3 INSERT LENGTHS TO ALLOW FOR 3 WEIGHT RANGES.
9-2-77

• A drawing illustrating the rocker arm/torsion bar suspension concept. This version utilized stock Allen wrenches for the torsion bars. Custom spring steel torsion bar axles were eventually developed and produced for the limited-production independent suspension truck.

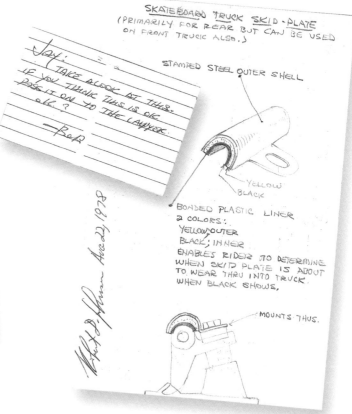

SKATEBOARD TRUCK SKID-PLATE (PRIMARILY FOR REAR BUT CAN BE USED ON FRONT TRUCK ALSO.)

JAY:
IF YOU THINK THIS IS OK — PASS IT ON TO THE LAWYER.
OK ?
— BOB

STAMPED STEEL OUTER SHELL

YELLOW
BLACK

BONDED PLASTIC LINER
2 COLORS:
YELLOW; OUTER
BLACK; INNER
ENABLES RIDER TO DETERMINE WHEN SKID PLATE IS ABOUT TO WEAR THRU INTO TRUCK WHEN BLACK SHOWS.

MOUNTS THUS.

Aug 22, 1978

• This "skid plate" concept, originally created to protect the truck while also providing a smooth steel grinding surface, was never developed. A simpler version, the Grindmaster, was later designed by Kevin Thatcher.

birth of a
SKATE ICON

By Jim Phillips

• Initial ideas for the Independent logo ranged from racing-inspired themes like checkered flags to global domination, sun globes, multi-directional arrows, and even an ankh. The surfer's good-luck cross proved to be the most powerful and rich in history.

One of my first jobs at NHS was designing logos and T-shirts for Road Rider Wheels. I was happy to have a steady account there, working on all the art-related projects they needed. When NHS decided to make their own trucks, Jay, Independent's mastermind, headed the design effort and had some engineers mock up prototypes with independent suspension, which was a radical concept.

When Jay asked me for a logo that would say "independent suspension," I went straight to my drawing board. I was working on a few sketches of the word "Indy" and criss-crossed racing flags when it hit me.

Skateboarding had evolved from sidewalk surfing and was still steeped in surf culture. I remembered the old "surfer's cross" that had been relegated to obscurity after the '50s. Since most of the early skaters were surfers, I figured it was seminal and germane to use this symbol. I sketched out the design in a circle shape to make it new, as the old Maltese cross that surfers and bikers had used in the '50s was squared off at the ends.

I went into NHS the next morning full of stoke, knowing it was a killer design. To my disappointment, my comp sketch went over like a lead balloon. Both Jay and Rich looked at it for a few minutes and pronounced it

22

> **"Independent has the ultimate icon in skateboarding."**
>
> —Eric Dressen

"too Nazi!" Sure, I protested, Germany used the symbol during the World Wars, but it was older and nobler than that. It was ancient Greek. It was the Lord's cross. It was an icon on shields and knights' armor during the Dark Ages. It appeared on every king's crown in feudal Europe. Christopher Columbus, backed by a world power, discovered America on ships displaying these giant crosses on their mainsails. It was a significant symbol, maybe the most powerful of all time.

But Jay and Rich were unmoved. Sadly, I went back to my studio, but I wasn't through. I went to my scrap file and looked for the Holy Grail that would convince them. Late that night, I found the deciding argument in my archives. At NHS early the next morning, I went in and stared at them for a moment. "Look," I said, and pulled out a *Time* magazine featuring the Pope. The Pope's hat and his robe's lapels were covered with rows of those little crosses. Jay and Rich smiled and looked at each other. "Well," they said, "if the Pope's got it, it must be okay!" We all laughed, and we had ourselves the beginnings of a logo.

Ever the meticulous businessman, Jay seized as much control of the logo as he had of the truck's mechanical prototyping. He put the initial

• Once convinced that the surfer's cross insignia would be the basis for the logo, Jay Shuirman took the concept to new heights by envisioning the addition of key pinlines and a color scheme that became Independent Truck Company's time-tested visual trademark.

sketch of the simple black rounded cross up on the wall and stared at it. "I see little pinlines around everything," he said. He sent me back to the drawing board, and I whipped up the first sticker design on art board with an ink pen, probably a Speedball B-2, loaded into a compass.

I worked with Jay's idea of writing "independent" flowing within the middle arms of the cross. Everything was symmetrical and geometric. I came up with the idea of crossing it with the word "suspension" with a common "e" in the center. Using my compass skills, I created little pinlines around, inside, and inside again. "Truck Company" appeared in a curve across the bottom. In those days, everything

was hand-lettered. I cut some color overlays, and this "Truck Co." logo sticker was slated to be printed on chrome Mylar in the good ol' red, black, and white.

To complete the decal series, we dropped the word "suspension" and added a few more internal lines. Jay looked through my Pantone color scale and picked the primary—blue, lime green, and yellow—and secondary colors for the next run of stickers.

Over the years, the Independent logo has stayed true to its origins and Jay's ideas. To this day, the original logo remains solid and traditional, tenaciously unchanged over the years. It is ubiquitous; it is heroic; it is

• A 1970s-era cover of *Time* magazine depicts Pope John Paul II with a Pallium— a series of four-sided crosses—on his garments. The red version at the bottom of his robe was the initial inspiration for Independent's icon.

BLACK
GREY
RED
ON WHITE

Independent. If I had a nickel for every Independent logo I've seen around the world, I'd be a happy man. But I would trade it all to have Jay back again.

"If the Pope's got it, it must be okay!"

—Jay Shuirman and Richard Novak

REBOUND

Ermico's second attempt at success in the skateboard market was the Rebound Truck. It was designed and produced by Ermico and distributed by NHS as part of their initial working relationship. Its double-cushion design was advanced in concept and influenced certain truck designs in the late '90s.

PRODUCTION STROKER

The production Stroker Truck was lighter than its initial prototype and more functional. Its intricate design and performance characteristics were unparalleled in high-speed downhill racing, but the design was too advanced for commercial acceptance.

THE 4 FOUNDERS MEET

The founders of Independent met at the Signal Hill downhill speed races of 1976. Ermico was there with the Stroker, and NHS was there with their advanced urethane wheel formulas. Their respective successes at this race brought them together to discuss advancing current truck designs. NHS had the functioning prototype torsion bar/rocker arm concept, and Ermico contributed development and production capabilities.

NHS P3

This fully functional prototype truck had a machined aluminum baseplate and a nylon hanger that housed the spring/rocker arm/axle suspension mechanisms. This design proved that the spring concept was too difficult to fine-tune and control.

NHS P4

Retaining the rocker arm design from the earlier prototypes, design efforts refocused on the torsion bar concept, which, was internalized this time inside the hanger utilizing a spring steel axle. Note the small pins that held the axle in place. This suspension mechanism proved to be the best design concept, but the actual truck design and turning geometry still needed major developing.

DARK GREEN
LIGHT GREEN
YELLOW
––––
ON WHITE

PROTOTYPE STROKER

Ermico's first product in the skateboard market was the Stroker Truck, resembling an automobile's suspension and undercarriage. This prototype Stroker was constructed from hand-welded steel and automobile-steering-inspired control arms.

STROKER HANGER & BASEPLATE MOLDS

These wooden molds fo[r] sand cast used to pour t[he] part of the Stroker's prod[uct] hangers and baseplates. Pictured above the hanger [&] baseplate are the holding units/display stands.

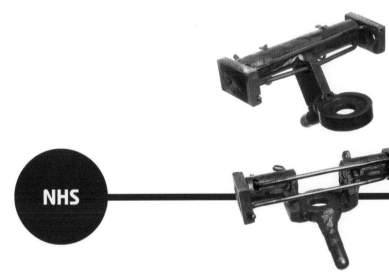

NHS P1

The first NHS suspension prototypes were hand welded and utilized a crude torsion bar and rocker arm axle concept. The prototypes shown here (front and rear) featured a split axle aligned with the kingpin.

NHS P2

When the first torsion bar concepts failed, the next prototypes featured spring-loaded rocker arms with multiple weight settings. The wooden model below the hand-welded prototype would have been used to produce sand-cast molds for a more developed prototype truck.

INDEPE

NDENT™

LIMITED PRODUCTION SUSPENSION

Further small refinements to the truck design and suspension mechanism resulted in the most successful truck ever produced for slalom racing. Only 12 original sets were made. Although many designers have tried to replicate this truck's performance, no one has mastered its secret design formula. Although this truck dominated the racing scene, it proved ineffective in bowls and pool riding. Efforts soon revolved around a straight-axle design.

PRODUCTION INDEPENDENT STAGE I

The truck that changed skateboarding forever.

THE INDEPENDENT BLOODLINE

Before their fateful introduction at Signal Hill, the founders of Independent were each developing their own truck designs: Ermico was experimenting with completely reinventing the conventional skateboard truck, while NHS was designing a suspension concept specifically for racing. By the time the four founders came together, each company had laid its own respective foundation for advanced skateboard truck design and development. The result of this merger was the first production skateboard truck, which could be easily adjusted, withstand a serious beating, and turn better than anything else available at the time.

BENNETT

The Bennett Truck had excellent turning characteristics, but its plastic baseplate broke easily, it was too tall, and the adjustment of its kingpin was problematic.

INDEPENDENT SUSPENSION PROTOTYPE

After developing the prototype Independent Truck to house the suspension configuration, a few sets of prototype suspension trucks were produced. Testing occurred for both bowl-riding and slalom-racing applications.

INDEPENDENT PROTOTYPE

This first prototype Independent was developed to house the suspension mechanism. It featured a hand-cast hanger and a distinctively shaped baseplate. This initial design and geometry are prevalent in all subsequent design stages.

TRACKER

The Tracker Truck design was durable and stable and could be adjusted easily, but it didn't offer quick turning characteristics for racing and bowl riding.

BASEPLATE MOLD

This Independent baseplate wooden model formed the sand-cast baseplate mold. Note the "patent pending" designation along the side of the baseplate.

If I Told You, I'd Have to Kill You— Tales From the Foundry

By C.R. Stecyk III

From 1981–1994, much of the development and production of Independent trucks originated inside the corrugated walls of building #275 in San Francisco's Hunter's Point Naval Shipyard.

United States Naval Shipyard, Hunter's Point, AAA Ship Fitters, Ermico Enterprises Incorporated, Casting Foundry: Building 275, San Francisco, California. What can I say to convey the ironies here? Having signed the non-disclosure agreements and still being bound to them, let's speak hypothetically. Imagine if the world's only dedicated skateboard truck foundry were situated smack in the middle of a top-priority defense facility. Independent meets the military industrial complex. Signs all over the base walls proclaim government logic: Loose lips sink ships. Do not ask—do not tell. What you see here, stays here. Trust no one. If I told you, I'd have to kill you. Military and authorized personnel only. No weapons, cameras, drugs, or alcohol. Access is controlled. Warning: armed patrols. Proceed only to area that you have been assigned.

Humor in uniform? Hardly. Ermico Enterprises Incorporated's unlikely home in the enterprise zone of the shadow warriors caused skate industrialists much worry. 131 Super Wides; 159 Fucking Wides; 169 Mother Fucking Wides; 215 Big Ten Inchers; Grindmaster Devices; Speed Rings; and Hollow Bodies were not marketing strategies or products in any con ventional sense. They were philosophical declarations of form and function. But oh, how industry honkers speculated and gossiped about them. How could they possibly have erected a 5,000-square-foot sheet metal Butler building in 48 hours? Why would Darrin Pelligro of the Dead Kennedys work as Eric Swenson's lead iron man? Didn't Gwynn Vitello, the gorgeous, intelligent, and capable genuine James Bond girl, work for San Francisco Mayors Alioto, Moscone, and Feinstein? Could Independent destroy the command and control center of the Golden Gate with its dereliction? Didn't Fausto, the same person who specialized in the study of Spanish Civil War anarchy for his college dissertation, actually get invited to Ronald Reagan and George Bush, Sr.'s inaugurations? Didn't the foundry have a super-stealthy section where Eric's technicians developed proprietary processes that were in fact being applied to frontline defense systems? Didn't Swenson date a submariner's daughter and dine with admirals at Dago Mary's?

The mysterious visitors and incidents at 275 fueled shipyard lore. Shore patrolmen were stupefied by the inherent energy and eccentricities of the Independent supernumeraries. Swenson manned the furnaces alone at three o'clock in the morning while playing his Gibson Custom through Marshall stacks loud enough to shake the buildings on the next dock. Olson forgot that he left his Raymond Lowey Studebaker President coupe there, rediscovered it eight years later, and then walked off again. (The Stude is still there.) Fausto used a five-story-high crane to move a massive 10-ton sand muller. Railroad cars dropped off top-grade metallurgical materials constantly, and just as swiftly, the foundry shipped tractor-trailer loads of Indys to NHS. (How many trucks were they making? Novak had to buy a 250,000-square-foot coastal cannery complex to accommodate his end of the distribution equation.) The crazier the antics, the more the production capability rolled. Three eight-hour shifts propelled the foundry 24 hours a

Clockwise from top left: *Swenson, Craig Stecyk, and Vitello (driving the forklift) relieve a sizeable test casting from its mold in Ermico's foundry; The first Independent truck ever produced; A truck hanger mold receives the placement of axle cores prior to casting; Baseplates and hangers get polished in the tumblers; In the machine shop, a hydraulic press pushes axles into the truck hangers.*

day. The business expanded into more and more buildings and built more furnaces. I slept away a portion of my life there on a bed of prime 356 aluminum ingots.

All highjinks aside, the foundry is the impenetrable aspect of the Independent mythos. It invokes the trucks' essential character, and its in-house capacities facilitate advanced testing and experimentation. The Independent clan has produced many breakthrough designs in response to changes they perceive in skateboarding's trajectory and riders' preferences. What the team learns in the field, the company implements immediately in its products. Any family member who has ever been allowed to glimpse EEI's Independent facility can attest to its state of the art supremacy. Rival truck competitors don't have a clue; they prefer to copy the original's geometry and farm out the casting to a variety of low-buck vendors and Third World sweatshops.

Glitches did arise, of course. Novak wouldn't talk to me for six months after one of my failed sculpture projects impeded Independent's production line. After Fausto encouraged me to get a "real job," I designed the Tracker man logo on his desk. Another bad one was the day I utilized Eric's drafting tools to knock out the first Venture logo. I may have been the biggest transgressor in a place where there were no saints. But fuck it. Family first. No one ever cared. No one did anything but laugh.

We invited pros who endorsed other trucks to visit, and we would use the Indy machine shop to try to modify the off-brand stuff to get it working a little better for them. Swenson and Vitello scratch-built custom trucks for Steve Rocco and Rodney Mullen because they needed designs to complement their distinctive skating styles, designs that weren't available elsewhere at the time. Indy launched a full-on R & D project to make those freestyle trucks for Steve and Rodney, in spite of the fact that both skaters were front men for other companies at that point. Try doing that anywhere else. Independent's open-door policy garnered scores of converts. Everyone lined up to get with the winning program.

Cooperation among fellow skaters and the acceptance of individual divergence are central tenets of the Independent philosophy. Everyone was generous to a fault, and acts of brotherhood were habitual. The boys gave Turnbull, the head shipyard security man, a perfect '59 Cad on his last day in service, "just so he could drive out with dignity." Swenson delighted in torturing me by making me drink port and smoke Habana Monte Cristos while I begged him for first-generation 215s. Somewhere—I don't know where, even though I've looked many times for it—he's got a stash of those suckers. He only pulls them out when he wants to watch people squirm.

In 1999 Eric and Fausto decided to redesign the operation by incorporating new manufacturing with research, development, warehousing, fabrication, casting, finishing, and shipping facilities all under a single 100,000-square-foot roof. This newest mega-manufacturing complex is next to the SFPD's Special Weapons and Tactics armory. The security around Ermico is good.

Built for Speed— Racing Domination

By John Hutson and Henry Hester

In 1976 and '77, I was fairly successful in the slalom and downhill skateboarding niche that I had carved out for myself. Racing was very pure; there was a clear winner and no subjective judging, and the fastest time took the prize. It was also a nice arena for product research and development, something NHS took very seriously in terms of wheel and deck design. Skateboard trucks were the company's next logical step.

My experience with Independent began in the spring of 1978. Richard and Jay asked me to meet two guys who had come down from San Francisco. I had a familiar initial reaction: "Here we go again ... some guys who don't ride skateboards are working on 'the next big thing,' bigger than the urethane wheel." Most of the new skateboard "inventions" I'd seen looked nothing like conventional skateboard trucks, and Fausto and Eric's design was no different. Their "Stroker" truck was an incredibly intricate concoction of swing arms, cams, levers, and ball joints. The thing looked like some strange steering component on a Formula One racecar. Unfortunately, these men were suffering from what I call "reinvention of the wheel disease."

Fausto and Eric were also refreshing, however, because they weren't the usual characters wanting to cash in on the latest wave of skateboarding. They were team mechanics for motorcycle racers and were adept at listening to test riders' analyses and making adjustments. They were also smart enough to see through my overly polite observations and realize I was not stoked on their trucks. I think there may have been one or two test sessions before the Stroker truck got stroked.

I preferred Bennett Trucks for racing because they had a tighter turning radius and weighed less than Trackers. The Indy founders were eager to observe Bennetts' advantages over

Trackers and to modify the easily breakable Bennett plastic baseplate. They recognized the necessity of developing a sturdy truck with a livelier—but not squirrelly—turning geometry and a beefiness that could withstand the constant grinding of modern-day pool riding.

Jay asked a retired master machinist named Clem Bricmont to contrive a mechanism that would allow each wheel to act independently of the other. Some dozen attempts at these trucks were fashioned from different springs, rods, welded pieces, and nylon hangers. The torsion bar concept was there, but none of these prototypes really worked. But when the founders worked together, magic happened, and the first true Independent Suspension Truck was born.

On a slalom course, the trucks' traction and stability were unequaled, and those who rode them ruled the events. At the time of my world-record-setting speed run in '78 at Signal Hill (at 53.45 miles per hour, it made the *Guinness Book of World Records* for fastest speed standing on a skateboard), I opted for a set of Indy 109s that were trimmed to remove weight. Presumably, the suspension would absorb momentum and reduce my top-end speed. Still, although slalom racers clamored for suspension trucks, the larger market was not amenable to such a product. The full-court press would be to market a conventional straight-axle truck, with the Independent name as its banner.

Around 1980, the idea of head-to-head downhill skateboard racing was taking hold with a small but devoted crew of enthusiasts. This racing style placed a premium on a rider's ability to draft another rider's slipstream, just as in NASCAR, one car pulls in directly behind

Above: *Olson blazes through a staggered arrangement of cones, September 1980.*
Opposite: *In his prize-winning speed tuck, John Hutson destroys the competition at Laguna Seca Speedway, July 1981.*

"...Independent was clearly out in front."
—John Hutson

Clockwise from top left: *Bob Denike races down the final 400 yards of Capitola's Monterey Avenue, September 1983; Hutson celebrates his victory at Capitola, August 1980; Sacramento's Don Bostick tucks towards the finish at Capitola, August 1980; Roger Hickey and Hutson battle for pink slips at Laguna Seca, July 1981; Judi Oyama decisively defeats Michelle Baker at Capitola, August 1980; A custom-helmeted Denike edges out Randy Katen in the home stretch, September 1981; Hutson and his daughter, Joanne, share some moments off course with Blackhart, September 1981.* Below: *Denike and Stecyk kick it on the sidelines between races, September 1981.*

The Capitola Classic

PROFESSIONAL
DOWNHILL
SKATEBOARDING

SEE THE THRILLS AND SPILLS OF
HIGH SPEED PROFESSIONAL SKATEBOARDING
GUARANTEED PURSE $1750

AUGUST 30 1980

CAPITOLA
99
CLASSIC

At Signal Hill in 1978, John Hutson became the fastest skateboarder in the world. With his then-unusual arms-back fairing technique referred to as the "Hut" tuck, he set a course that many racers have tried to achieve. Burning urethane in its truest form at Laguna Seca, CA, September 1980.

another and gets sucked along, gaining enough momentum to slingshot past the competitor.

The Capitola Classic head-to-head race took place in the center of town, near Santa Cruz. In early years, it was a simple, single-lane slalom race—a grassroots deal that was a huge hit with the local crowds. The idea of a head-to-head race, with two riders on one course, was irresistible to riders and spectators. The need for speed was taking over everywhere. Laguna Seca, in Monterey, California, and Bellevue, Washington both offered courses with higher speeds (up to 45 miles per hour).

Most of the riders in slalom competitions joined the downhill movement, as well as a good showing of top bowl and pool riders who loved the guts/balls aspect of these wild, head-to-head races. The Independent trucks designed for wider decks proved just right for downhill speed, affording riders the requisite stability and handling for head-to-head competition. While other trucks were out there, Independent was clearly out in front.
—John Hutson

It was 1978, and we were in Akron, Ohio at an event slated to be a "world championship" competition, which every other big contest was billed

as at the time. The top players in the Giant Slalom were all there, including Bob Skoldberg, John Hutson, and me. The event represented a milestone for product development, as faster equipment was not only emerging weekly but was also essential for winning.

Unfortunately for the rest of the racers, a few of us were privileged enough to get either a full set, or at least one, of the new Independent Suspension Trucks. Hutson, Skoldberg, Terry Brown, and I each had one of these custom-made trucks on the rear of our board. Everyone else at the race was running dry. Needless to say, we were in heaven, and they were pissed.

The theory of the Independent Suspension Truck was basic: the rocker arms flexed as you rode so the wheels wouldn't spin out, especially in the back. This allowed us to ride faster, harder wheels in the front and in the back, something the others couldn't do with their straight-axle trucks. The difference between Indys and traditional trucks was amazing—so much so that by the time we got to Akron, using Indys was considered cheating by the "have nots," who attempted to have them banned. It felt like cheating, and it felt really good. From that contest forward, Independent Suspension Trucks had it going on and owned the top three spots in racing. It cracked me up. —Henry Hester

"It felt like cheating, and it felt really good." —Henry Hester

Below, left to right: *During practice heats, Hutson runs the cones at Akron, OH, July 1978; Contemporaneous racing equipment, August 1978; Racers Jamie Hart, Cliff Coleman, John Krisick, Mike Goldman, and Hutson geared up at Signal Hill, June 1978.*

The Day Independent Arrived

Hester Pro Bowl Series Contest #3, Ride On Skatepark, Newark, CA, May 23, 1978

Ground Zero:
Newark, CA, 5-23-78

By Bob Denike

Recorded history places the commercial arrival of Independent in Northern California at the Newark Pro Bowl contest in May 1978. Now backtrack about 12 months to the initial development and riding of a full-suspension slalom truck, along with a few loose meetings in Santa Cruz and San Francisco to pinpoint its actual conception. Four men met to talk about a better skateboard truck. They stumbled upon an indelible brand.

The key ingredients were two motorcycle race mechanics, two guys with a skateboard company, a handful of renowned team riders, and a powerful icon. The founders were innately skilled at promotion, distribution, and product design and production. Perfect time, perfect mix, perfect recipe for success … or perhaps disaster. But Independent prevailed; though unknown at the time, it would become the focal point of a subcultural movement and shape skateboarding as we know it today.

Independent came on like an electrical storm—low and buzzing. It seemed suddenly to have always been there, rolling in like a slow fog,

creeping into skateboarding at a time when something dark just felt necessary. It felt like the color black. It was dirty, leathery, and raw. It felt illegal and greasy. If you hung your head over the fence of the Newark keyhole pool that day, you could just feel things begin to change. Whispers and rumors circulated in the bleachers; shadowy figures distributed stuff from the trunk of a beat-up car. Who were these guys, who was riding the trucks, what did the name and logo mean? It was just too much to swallow.

The team's moves were powerful that day, and not coincidentally. The guys riding the trucks were just so far ahead, achieving the first frontside roll-in on vert, the beginnings of the frontside layback, and the first handplant ever. For the first time in competition, tricks were happening above the lip and outside the bowl. And in transcending the physical restraints of their terrain, the skateboarders simultaneously liberated themselves from the confines of the skateboarding industry at the time.

"Our heads spun, trying to digest what we were witnessing that day..."

—Bob Denike

Clockwise from top left: *Blackhart's frontside airs played a vital role in his dialed lines; Depiction of a teenage Rubberman; NorCal's Brian Buck grinds the newly poured and obtrusive coping during the preliminary rounds; Jim Muir, Kim Cespedes, Ray Allen, and Olson check the heat sheets.*

Opposite page: *In front of a lineup of shutterbugs, newly recruited Indy rider Bobby Valdez drifts a frontside air above Darrell Miller to secure second place during the heated doubles event.*

Previous spread: *The skaters and spectators in this photograph witnessed many memorable moments over this weekend, including the first public appearance of Independent Truck Company's high-performance trucks and bold logo. The newly created team of riders surpassed all others in its first outing for a bowl riding competition.*

Skateboarding was at a crossroads. As freestyle skating and slalom racing gasped their last breaths, the future—vertical pool skating—loomed large. Seemingly overnight, the boards got fatter, the trucks got wider, and the moves got bolder. Very few companies could meet demands for better products. Container loads of skateboard product and hundreds of pro skateboarders became obsolete.

As our heads spun, trying to digest what we were witnessing that day at the Newark pool, we became vulnerable to a new force in skateboarding. Independent slapped the sport in a better direction; it freed us from structure and team jerseys. Skateboarding was a virgin before that. It went in drinking soda and left the place with booze. Like the first smoke you actually enjoy, Independent enters your veins and never quite filters itself out. Skateboarding went underground that day. Independent had arrived.

Suspended in what is perhaps the most striking and gnarly photo session of its time, Steve Alba precariously soars frontside over Scott Dunlap's backside carve above the Pipeline Skatepark's vertically endowed 15-foot bowl, February 1979.

1978-1981

The Crash, the Revolution, and Going Underground ✠✠✠✠

By Bob Denike

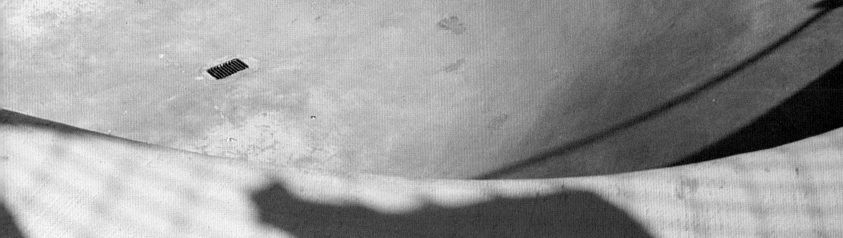

Throughout 1978 and into '79, the Independent machine never let up. Things were moving fast, with new riders and products stampeding into the fold. Deck widths increased rapidly from six to eight, and then 10 to 11, inches, and the team wanted wider trucks to match. Independent delivered promptly by releasing new widths every month.

At an even greater rate, bowl riding pros were signing on. Following Olson, Blackhart, KT, Salba, Malba, the Buck Brothers, and Bobby Valdez were Brad Bowman, Kevin O'Regan, Howard Hood, Peter "Kiwi" Gifford, Rod Saunders, Kevin Moore, Doug Saladino, Scott Foss, and Darrell Miller. The top guys simply knew they were getting involved in something that was going in the right direction.

The sudden appearance of Independent and its subsequent takeover of the balance of 1978 were mirrored by another fateful event: the peak, and then the rapid demise, of the entire skateboard industry.

When the July '78 issue of *Skateboarder* magazine landed in mailboxes across the US, it bore an ominous message. "Big Summer Issue" sprawled across the cover of the magazine's largest release to date. Inside coverage revolved around skatepark construction and reported one contest after another. The format of the issue foretold the sport's disintegration; when a skateboarding magazine starts to feel more like a phonebook, moving from one contest to the next and corralling kids behind chain-link fencing, watch out, 'cause it's due for a downturn. Sure enough, after its peak following the Newark Hester contest, the biz took a sliding dump. By February '79, outdated pros and fly-by-night companies that pumped out ill-conceived product littered the roadside.

By late spring of '79, skateparks had multiplied like fertile rabbits, topping off at about 400 facilities across the US. Most couldn't survive, however; bad design, injury litigation, and kids unwilling to "pay to play" took their toll, and the parks began closing as quickly as they had opened. They started out as the "future of skateboarding" and ended under the blade of the bulldozer. Jerry "Taters" Hurtado, the manager of the Big O Skatepark at the time, remembers, "Every parent of a kid with a broken femur or wrist wanted to grab a lawyer and sue for the one-mil cashout. Plus, most of the park designs were crap. Guys who had never stepped on a board or even cared were laying cement." Still, the super-talented skaters kept improving and pulling ahead of those less skilled in the process; you either kept up or were forced to sit down and watch. Kids were over it. By the beginning of the '80s, existing skateparks had dwindled to less than a dozen.

Skateboarder magazine drove yet another nail into the coffin during this period. Curtis Hesslegrave, then the associate editor of the mag, recalls, "We really shot ourselves in the foot. We let the bulk of people who were skateboarding go in favor of pool riding, not realizing that most people in the US did not have access to an empty swimming pool. Many of the other forms of skateboarding—slalom, freestyle, downhill, and skating on natural terrain—were forced to take a back seat to vertical bowl riding."

Hesslegrave continues, "In 1979, when Warren Bolster ran the magazine, he was showing all aspects of skateboarding, and we enjoyed across-the-spectrum participation. When the new editor, Brian Gillogly, took over, he focused the mag strictly on pool riding for the next two years. The net result was a huge attrition of kids from skateboarding; if you weren't a pool rider, you weren't a skateboarder, and that killed it. Skateboarding didn't come back until it came back in the streets."

Amid all this doom and gloom, however, punk rock and new wave music invaded, igniting a subcultural revolution that would change skateboarding's style forever. Many remember Steve Olson as the first skate punk, whose trips to Ermico and to punk clubs in SF with Fausto, Terry Nails and the crew inspired him. Hurtado says, "Olson was like a stepchild back then, when there weren't too many punkers around. He was the champ at the time, a major influence who inadvertently turned the skate world on to punk. I remember seeing him go from surf rat to punk rat, with a leather jacket and checkerboard flat top." Olson's influence caught the industry off guard, but while many of the "uptights" questioned his professionalism and its effect on skateboarding, the kids knew better. They were ripe for change.

Hurtado continues, "Independent had this 'fuck you' attitude—let skaters be skaters—and the skaters they chose to ride for them reflected that philosophy. Punk caught on quickly. SF had a great punk club scene, and the guys there embraced it; Olson was first, and then Salba, Alva, Bowman, and Duane followed. D.P. was a major punk influence, too."

The rawness of skateboarding and the rawness of punk rock appeared to be naturally harmonious. The skaters who survived skateboarding's late '70s downfall were branded as outcasts in the '80s, and they found a perfect outlet in the music, which was pissing people off left and right. The prevailing notion was, "They already hate us; let's piss them off even more!" And so, in a firestorm that seemed to catch overnight, skaters abandoned Van Halen, Led Zeppelin, Foghat, Ted Nugent, Boston, and AC/DC and discovered Devo, The Damned, The Clash, The Ramones, 999, and The Sex Pistols. Adults couldn't understand, but the kids were eating it up. Hurtado adds, "I used to make tapes in '79 and play them at the Big O Skatepark, and I'd get so much flak from parents. It was just too much for the moms. You would play some Ramones, like 'Beat on the Brat,' and they're all stressed out, asking, 'What is this music about? I don't want my child listening to this!'" As skaters' musical tastes became even more core, The Dead Kennedys, X, The Germs, and Black Flag were added to the playlist.

Spurred on by the smoldering remnants of an industry and a group of skaters unwilling to quit, the next stage—street skating—ushered in yet another major phase in skateboarding's history. As the parks closed, skateboarding returned to its roots, rediscovering ditches, schoolyards, streets, and driveways. Ever the evolutionist, Steve Olson, along with Independent and Santa Cruz Skateboards, embraced the shift, placing the first "street skating" ad in February 1980, with the tagline "Free on the Streets" clearly summing up the times and setting the direction for the future. Hurtado explains, "The combination of punk rock and street skating bred a different type of skater: a guy who didn't need the norm, didn't need the rules and restrictions, didn't need the equipment and the lifetime park pass. All he needed was his leather jacket, his 501s, his Chuck Taylors, and a street skate. It could have been a marketing move, but at the same time, it was inevitable. You had to go back to whatever was there before."

Throughout 1980, though, the skateboarding world continued to slash, crash, and burn. *Skateboarder* magazine had morphed into a pre–X Games event program called *Action Now* magazine, and true skateboarders felt abandoned. *Skateboarder* was telling the world it no longer looked at skateboarding as a viable industry that could float its own boat, and *Action Now* was a weak-ass attempt to branch out and grab a larger advertising revenue base. Those who stuck around knew it was wrong.

Why share the stage with pedals, water, and snow? Skaters wanted their own magazine and their own industry, and they demanded their own voice. After canvassing the remaining Southern California skate companies for support (and meeting rejection at every turn), Fausto and the remaining founders of Independent joined Kevin Thatcher and Ed Riggins and launched *Thrasher* magazine in January 1981. The magazine had to happen; those who continued to skate knew that they couldn't allow skateboarding to die or play second fiddle to anything less intense. The industry shifted its focus to *Thrasher* in less than six months, and *Action Now* closed up shop in August 1981.

Excerpts from an editorial in the maiden issue of *Thrasher,* by Editor Kevin Thatcher, set the tone for the future and defined a lifestyle that many were not willing to abandon:

"At the height of the skatepark explosion in the late '70s, skaters were virtually swept off the streets and deposited in the parks. The action was radical but lacked the intensity of a knock-down, drag-out backyard pool session or a skate cruise down the boulevard. The fact is, skateboarding can survive without skateparks, but the parks will never last without skaters. Street skating is fun and also visual. The whole world is out there waiting to be entertained, but they want it delivered to their doorstep. So let's deliver! *Thrasher* was born out of an activity that has established itself as a major pastime for many people and a rewarding experience for countless others. 'Thrashing' is an attitude, a skate attitude. Thrashing is part of a lifestyle, a fast-paced feeling to fit this modern world. Thrashing is finding something and taking it to the limit—not dwelling on it, but using it to its fullest and moving on. Skateboarding has not yet reached its maximum potential, and who can say what the limits are? To find out—grab that board! You don't have to be a super-talented professional skater. Grab that board—if you're a novice having some fun on a Saturday afternoon. To the kid hanging out at the Stop 'N' Shop with his gang—grab that board! There are no rules saying that you have to go fast or skate vertical. There is tons of asphalt and concrete being poured every day, so—grab that board!"

After the launch of *Thrasher,* skateboarding, existing solely in its rawest forms, rooted itself firmly in the underground of the early '80s. Schoolyard banks, urban and suburban street areas, downhill runs, spillways and ditches, pipes, backyard pools, and scrap-plywood unified a small, yet global, community of hardcore skateboarders. They rode what was available, and they did so because it was in their blood. And Independent was right there the whole time—unfazed, continuing to adapt, and gaining loyalty like no other skateboard company.

Pulling out modern moves, Micke Alba snaps a frontside ollie during "Devo Day" at Pomona Pipe and Pool Skatepark, September 1979.

"Ironically, the move toward more aggresive bowl riding was a boost for Independent's momentum and, at the same time, a catalyst for the start of skateboarding's demise."

—Bob Denike

*Blackhart hits a full-tilt frontside wheeler at Lakewood,
well before the lights were plugged in, July 1978.*

rick
BLACKHART ✠ ✠ ✠ ✠

Left to right: *Laid-back street cruisin'*,
*1981; Before there were beer bongs,
there was Blackhart, April 1979;
FSU, MFW, 1980.*

"I want to know the history of skateboarding.
These idiots today don't want to know shit." —Rick Blackhart

From his skating roots in San Jose and as a local at the secretive Los Altos Pool and the nearby 30-foot Bombora fullpipe, Rick Blackhart's progress in skateboarding came naturally. By 1978, Rick was one of the top pro riders, and he put Northern California on the skateboarding map as a force to be reckoned with.

In his short career as a pro, Blackhart carried himself like a rock star. He was known for his spontaneous and Gumby-ish style, which earned him the nickname "Rubberman." He shunned the trappings of a pro career and often went on the road to ride pipes in Texas and the Arizona desert or to get loose with friends at pools and parks in California. Rick embodied the NorCal bad-boy attitude; he was banned for life from Winchester Skatepark and its perfect keyhole pool for throwing a flawless, 50-yard spiral football through the front window. Along the way, he picked up another nickname, "Doctor Rick," for his extensive knowledge of the various recreational pharmaceuticals prevalent in skateboarding in the late '70s.

Rick lived in the shadows of skateboarding until he blasted onto the scene at Newark in '78, taking third in the overall Hester Series standings. Blackhart remembers:

"The mornings of the Newark contest, we were going to this backyard pool in Gilroy. You had to skate it at five in the morning and leave by seven. It was the only time you could ride it without a bust going down. Rather than start in the shallow end, I learned to roll in backside over the coping from the deck of the pool. That pool was built for roll-ins. It had this coping that was flat on top, like a modern roll-out deck, and the transition was killer. I

would just skate along the edge backside and drop in. No one was doing roll-ins back then, and I soon learned to roll out and then roll back in, in one fluid motion. So we would go in the morning to skate the Gilroy Pool and then move on to Newark in the afternoon to practice for the contest. Newark wasn't an easy bowl to roll into; it had a lot of steep wall and two feet of vert, and it was shaped more like a kettle. A lot of guys were soon rolling out as well, but they wouldn't roll back in; instead, they would ride over to the channel and roll back down the channel into the bowl. I did pretty well in the Newark prelims and made the final cut, scoring some points and attention with my backside roll-out and -in.

"The day of the finals, Kevin Thatcher and I and a few other guys went to the Gilroy Pool. I knew I had to learn something that no one else was doing; that would seal the deal and put me in first place. The first frontside roll-in I ever did was that morning at Gilroy, and I did it later that same day in the contest. It was my second and final run. I rolled out frontside along the lip. The crowd behind the fence was grabbing me and yelling and shit. I kept rolling closer and closer to the channel hip, looking for a place to drop in. I ran out of deck and just hopped in and fell all the way to the bottom of the transition, landing and pumping toward the next wall. That was it right there. I thought the judges had to give it to me; the crowd was going crazy. I thought it was over. Everyone was going, 'Dude, you won, you won!' I just had to wait for them to tally it up and get my trophy and my money, and I was out of there. After a few minutes of chaos and the judges talking, they tell me I tied with someone, asking me what I would think if there was a tie. 'That would be fucked. That's pussy shit.' I was pissed off, and I told them,

43

A road trip to Arizona's desert pipes finds Dr. Rick well above the vertical markers on this frontside thruster, September 1978.

'Make a decision and pick a fucking winner!' The head judge came back out and said Bobby Valdez had won.

"For me, that was the beginning of power versus trick skating. That shit has gone on for years: Rick Blackhart vs. Bobby Valdez; Duane Peters vs. Eddie Elguera; Christian Hosoi vs. Tony Hawk; Tony Trujillo vs. whoever; on and on. There were two styles of skating; one was where you try to think what you're going to do and try to do exactly what you are thinking about and don't do anything else. That was a big thing back then. My style of skating was, you dropped in and had no clue what you were going to do or where. As soon as you did your first wall move, you would pump into the second and see where you were, working with your body position to just keep going. 'Okay, I have enough speed, so I'll go backside … whoa, I got thrown off, so now I'll just lipslide.' If your line took you somewhere, you would just go with it. Everyone thought my style was more fluid. I remember guys saying, 'He can almost eat shit and make something out of it and keep going.' The judges didn't catch on to that; the skating was too hard to judge 'cause it was different every time, but that's how I skated. Fuck them.

"I was at NHS one day, and Jay said, 'I'm going to have a meeting with these two guys. Why don't you come upstairs and talk to them about trucks?' And there were Eric and Fausto. All I could think was that Jay and Novak were totally joking and setting me up. Jay was the master of the straight face and was always kidding around. I was just thinking, 'You want me to fucking talk to these guys?' They were greasers with long hair, moustaches, wife beater T-shirts, and dirty jeans. I'm looking at Eric and Fausto and wondering, 'Can you two guys be any more scummy? You guys can't be for real.'

"Jay and Rich had been fooling around with truck designs and wanted Eric and Fausto to produce the truck. We got to talking about what they were all going to do and what they had planned, and Fausto was just going off, talking about the need for wider trucks and all. Days before we sealed the deal for me to test the first Independent prototypes, I got a shirt and a set of trucks from Tracker. I was hunting around for a truck sponsor, and Tracker was the only real game in town at the time. I remember Jay and Fausto just hassling me, asking, 'You get any money? You agree to anything?' 'No, they just gave me a shirt and a pair of trucks.' 'Well, fuck that shit; you don't ride that shit anymore. We're gonna do something different.' And that was it. I rode for Independent."

—B.D., from an interview with Rick Blackhart

Clockwise from top left: *Spit gutter–edge play at Mills High School pool, July 1978; Poppin' the clutch, March 1980; Tuckin' for bucks in Capitola, August 1980; With glue-foot mastery, Rick inadvertently lays down a rail and drives a dodgy backside roll-in with success at the Big O capsule, July 1978.*

OLSON ✠ ✠ ✠ ✠

"Old school? New school? Fuck school." —Steve Olson

Steve "Bulky" Olson has logged more time on a skateboard than most professional skateboarders can shake a stick at. He'll skate anything on any pretense and tell you how he thinks it is, even if you don't ask or want to know. Here's the story, according to Olson:

"Around the time of the Hester Series in 1978, the Independent founders gave Blackhart and me each a set of suspension trucks. I said, 'Well, that's a great idea if you are into racing, but we're here to take the fuckin' coping off, and those trucks don't work for fuckin' skateparks. Give me back my ACS 650s, 'cause I got a contest to skate in, and get these fuckin' rocker arm things the fuck off. Lose the suspension and make it wider, and you got a sick truck.' That was it. I don't recall who the fuck came up with the Independent truck idea, but I do recall that in *Skateboarder* mag's 'Who's Hot' article about me, there's a little quote about how it would be a smart idea to have a strong baseplate and the turning radius of a fuckin' Bennett truck. It was pretty simple.

"I just thought that it was cool that Fausto, Swenson, Novak, and Shuirman wanted to build a truck that really worked and turned super fuckin' good. So at the Newark Hester Contest, when Indy hit the scene, and when most of us were just a bunch of surfer kids that rode skateboards, it was a big deal. The team back then consisted of me, Blackhart, Salba, Valdez, Bowman, and the racers: Hutson, Hester, Goldman, and whoever else. We had some badass motherfucking skateboarders. That was also when I saw Terry Nails dressed all punk rock like, and that changed my life. Thanks, Nails; I owe you something. Indy and punk rock hit skateboarding around the same time, and although the boys at NHS didn't get the punk rock thing at all, the boys at Ermico did, and being located in SF and knowing Terry Nails didn't hurt, either.

"In those days, you couldn't get away with just riding the street. You had to be able to hook up at any spot and all-around rip, no matter what. Hosoi was a kid who could skate fuckin' everything; he was the last of the fuckers who really ripped.

"The evolution of skateboarding is part of what makes it so amazing. Tell a guy who studies gravity about the ollie air, and he'll tell you it's not possible on Earth. Then show him a kid who can ollie 24 stairs with a kickflip. And what about street style? I want to see some guy do a fuckin' layback, dragging his head down the rail on a 35-stair fucker. Let's get a little wild out there, like Trujillo. He knows how to draw lines and flow. It shouldn't be like going up to the top, throwing a heelflip, and then stopping. Stop? Pick up your board and turn around? What the fuck is wrong with you? You got 45 seconds. You should be able to keep going, faster and faster with each trick, and make all your tricks.

"When I was younger, we got paid 50 dollars a week to skateboard; it wasn't about the money. When you ask pros today, and even some amateurs, if they want to go skating, they'll reply, 'Yeah, let me go call my photographer.' What the fuck is that? When kids start skateboarding now, at first they do it for fun, and then they start getting in magazines and getting paid, and that's cool, too. But all of a sudden, they start wondering, 'Am I selling enough boards?' and it's like a profession. What about just fucking rolling? Do you skateboard for fun or do you skateboard so you can get high, get paid and go and get filmed and see yourself in the magazine? Skateboarding is still sweet, but the business is fucked. Money ruins the whole world.

"My son is a skateboarder, but he's not the type of kid to say, 'This is my dad; he used to be a pro skateboarder.' He knows I didn't use to be a skateboarder; I'm still one. You wanna race? Let's race, you little shit! You

Olson's frontside floater casts an iconic shadow under a tall transition at High Roller in Phoenix, AZ, December 1978.

This page, clockwise from top left: *Tearing into America's heartland with a backside air at Apple Skatepark in Columbus, OH, December 1979; Olson's self-made skate-punk couture and attitude put heat in the streets, May 1979; On course at Marina Del Rey's banked slalom, December 1979; Jetsetting through LAX, Feb 1979; Olson was an early practitioner of the rock and roll, Winchester, August 1978.*

Opposite page, top: *Channels were originally designed to facilitate rolling into bowls well before it became routine to jump across them. Olson hucks and tucks a frontside channel flight at the Big O pro-am contest. He hung up upon reentry, made it, and squashed the competition, February 1980.*
Bottom: *Punk before you ever thought you were, February 1980.*

wanna ride a pipe? Let's go ride a pipe. Let's see if you can grind a fuckin' pool. He's the kind of kid who actually has a soul. He doesn't like to get filmed because he doesn't think he's good enough, or at least he has the integrity to stop and say, 'Well, I'm not that good yet.'

"Little kids are way cooler than teenagers. They're still stoked on skateboarding. You can go and hang out with eight-year-olds and have better conversations with them than you can with a 16-year-old kid who thinks he's all that. The little kid will look at you and think, 'You're 40 years old, and you still skateboard. That means when I'm your age, I can still skateboard.' But the little asshole who's 16 is like, 'Pffft, I just did a nollie heelflip, fuckin' backside boardslide, 180 out. What can you do?' Well, fuck, little kid, you weren't even a little sperm cell in your dad's nut bag when we were cracking our heads open learning ollie airs. And these kids are the ones that are fuckin' going to keep this sport going?

"I really don't give a fuck, though; I'll still be skateboarding when I'm 60. I'll be able to go down a hill at 45 mph because they'll have detachable knees and shit … and leathers."

—*B.D., from an interview with Steve Olson*

"I don't know if the average kid will ever understand Steve Olson. He's a true skateboarder, not just doing tricks. Skateboarding isn't about doing tricks; it's about standing on the board and rolling. He's always flowing. It's a language for him." —Mark Gonzales

Left and right: Following a heavy slam, Salba receives comfort and a butterfly bandage from his dad and Gwynn Vitello in his bedroom, March 1980. Center: The Alba sons and mom suited up for Skateboarder *magazine's Rider Poll Awards, December 1978.*

ALBA ✠ ✠ ✠ ✠

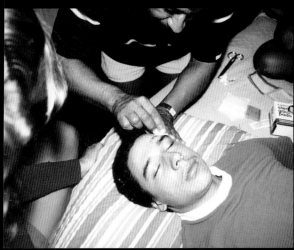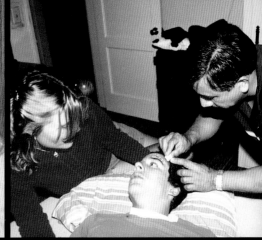

"The Hell's Angels have Harley-Davidson. We have Independent." —Steve Alba

For me, it all started at the third contest of the Hester Series, up at Ride On Skatepark in Newark, California (NorCal). I had previously won the Spring Valley contest and had done decently at Upland. I was really practicing for Newark, learning backside airs, flowing around, and carving hard, with a couple of slides mixed in after a frontside air for good measure. Remember, kiddies: there really were no established tricks yet. Blackhart introduced the roll-in—frontside, I believe—at Newark and just blew minds. At the same contest, Bobby Valdez brought out the first invert, which was really insane. The bowl only had a channel entrance, so you had to be a snake and a half to get any runs. Everybody showed up for this contest, because the park had just been built, and it offered more of a pool-like structure and had a coping lip (coping was key) with a flat-topped deck.

We flew up the day before the contest, and all the skaters stayed in the same hotel, which just got trashed because the hellions all got into water fights ... followed later by food fights at some Chinese restaurant. The day before the contest, Blackhart and Olson were raving about these new skateboard trucks called Independent; they had been created initially for downhill and slalom, but new castings just for bowl riding were also being developed. Blackhart and Olson were the only guys riding the trucks at that point. I was riding Trackers with longer axles and a bearing spacer on each side of the axle to make the grinding surface wider.

Later that day, these two scruffy bearded guys in grease-covered Levi's walked up to me out of the blue and introduced themselves as Fausto and Eric. They asked if I would try their trucks. My setup was critical in those days, and I really didn't want to be bothered, but I told them that as long as they set up my board just as it was, I would try them. I heavily doubted their abilities. But they came back half an hour later, and the board was just like I had it set up. So Mr. V and Swenson got it just right, and my board actually still rolled straight. I told them to give me an hour to scope the trucks. They said if I liked 'em, I could ride for Independent, and they would pay me, like, 25 to 50 bucks a month.

I gave them a shot, and I could not believe how rad they turned. Up until then, I had tried every truck imaginable: Suregrip, Bennett, ACS, Lazer, Gull Wing, and Trackers. I loved Indy trucks in that first half-hour. I could turn so well, I was pulling figure-eight carves in the bowl. Nobody else could actually carve the bowl like that without lifting up his front wheels. People did figure eights, but not true ones like I was doing. That was all it took; I was hooked.

I never looked back. Everybody who saw the Indy crew wanted those damn trucks, and I swear, Olson and Blackhart and I had an edge on everybody because of those trucks. It was history in the making.

Fausto and Eric were asking all kinds of dudes to try the trucks, and Dave Dominy from Tracker was getting hella chapped on them for stealing riders. Bobby Valdez was another convert that day at the contest, and a lot of NorCal guys got on the team soon after that. Team Indy was born at Newark. Look at Blackhart's ad; it's his roll-in from that very day. "Fucking hot!!!" was the caption, and the Indy image was born.

The next contest of the series was at the Big O, and I won in the 115-degree SoCal heat. By then, lots of people were riding Indys; the company had the image, the position, and the balls to say fuck you to everybody.

Controlled above three feet of vertical, Salba takes charge on an edgy frontside wheeler at the Pipeline, July 1979.

Their punk attitude really did wonders for me back then. Everybody in the skate world told me that I was a fluke, but I came back hard and won with frontside and backside airs, channel airs, slides, bert reverts, and roll-ins that I learned from Blackhart. Those were the raddest times for sure, and still no flippity trickery yet … just pure flow.

The best thing of all, though, was going up north to hang with Fausto and his beautiful wife, Gwynn, at their house. She worked for San Francisco's Mayor Feinstein, and she always hooked up the raddest concert tickets for anything going on in the city. We saw bands at The Mab like The Avengers, The Dils, The Nuns, DOA, Flipper, and Devo. This was when punk was champion, and all the new rad skaters on the Indy team got into punk rock in search of new attitudes for the climate of social change. We were at the forefront of teenage anarchy and chaos. During those years, I saw many shows up in the city and met many new friends who skated and were also into this new phenomenon.

At one point, the whole Indy team was up north for a contest at Winchester, and we all went out later that night to see The Clash, The Dead Kennedys, and The Cramps at the Temple Beautiful (where Jim Jones used to preach). We took over the place like nothing you have ever seen. By random chance, skaters made up slamdancing that night, trying to get onstage, all liquored up and clad in black leather jackets and purple Converse high tops. Punk rock has never been the same.

Back then, the skateparks up north were not too shabby. Winchester ruled, and Milpitas was also pretty damn rad. I met all kinds of cats, all tried and true Indy riders: Mofo and K.T., Scotty Parsons, Kevin Reed, Jim Martino, the Buck "Bunk" Brothers, Robert "The Fly" Schlafly, Peter "Kiwi" Gifford, Bob Denike, Eric Halverson, Tim Lockfelt (who saw The Pistols' last show at Winterland and wore the hand-screened leopard-skin shirt that I bugged and begged him for), Joe Fong, Scott Foss, Randy "Skatin'" Katen, B.K., Don "Fish" Fisher, and others.

I can't say enough about how appreciative I am for Fausto's inspiration all these years or about how punk he and Eric were, starting their own magazine, *Thrasher,* after *Skateboarder* and *Action Now* took a shit. They helped us travel, covered contest entry fees, and paid us way back when nobody did. I know lots of people have been bitter over the years for not receiving what they felt was coming to them, but I look at it this way: since 1978, I have never had to pay for any trucks, magazines, wheels, clothes, or anything affiliated with the northern connection.

To this day, I still don't get paid, but that has never ruined my love of skateboarding. Money is not the reason I began skating. I won't ever quit Indy and go to another truck company, like a whole bunch of other people who will ride whatever rubbish is out there. It's either Indy all the way or nothing at all. It's an attitude, and it's more like a family than anything else. Would you bail out on your family just for money? That's all bullshit.

Skateboarding is freedom of expression, and I love the adrenaline rush that it gives me. I have always been stoked to be one of the original guys who still skates, and I'm proud to be part of the family that originated that afternoon back at Newark. I have nothing but praise for Mr. V and Mr. Swenson for sticking up for all of us skaters and looking out for me all these years. Team Indy forever! —*Steve Alba*

"Indy originally was this core group of skaters who were all anti-establishment. They had this attitude, 'We don't care about anybody, we got our own little thing, we're into this new thing called punk rock....' The whole punk rock attitude mixed with skating was Independent."

—Steve Alba

Clockwise from top left: *Salba follows through on a low-slung frontside grind revert at Boulder, CO, July 1979; Never mind the freestylers and Varibots, here's Salba, July 1979; Nocturnal rock and roll slider at Colton, April 1981; Salba tears into the coping-less lip at the Runway in Carson, CA, November 1978.*

"Nothing turns like an Indy." —Steve Alba

Clockwise from top: *Barging Skate City's reservoir in creepers, March 1981; Teenage rebellion at Winchester, August 1978; During the Gold Cup Series, La Machine jumps the channel at the Big O, July 1980.*

"The one picture where Duane has the bleach-blond hair, Bermuda shorts, spiked wristband, crouched-down street shot, I think that one is an Independent trademark, something you remember forever about Indy." —Mark Gonzales

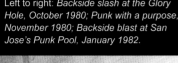

Left to right: *Backside slash at the Glory Hole, October 1980; Punk with a purpose, November 1980; Backside blast at San Jose's Punk Pool, January 1982.*

"independent has always been punk rock." —Duane Peters

I first met Fausto and Eric at Oasis Skatepark in the late '70s. I was trying to get my shit back together after a three-month hospital ordeal. As I began riding the pool, these two loud guys with moustaches yelled at me to come over. They were really curious about where I had gotten the Indy trucks, and what I thought of them, and also whether I was the kid who did the "El Rollo." After we exchanged some words, they gave me some newer trucks, which were wider than the norm, and some killer stickers. At that time, most of the people in the industry didn't really seem to give a shit about skating, and they for sure didn't care about the "always-more-than-expendable loser" riding their products. I was blown away that these two dude mans gave a shit about my opinion of how the trucks turned and whether they could be lighter without losing strength. I got 10th at Oasis, and Fausto called my house when I got home, asking, "Do you want to ride for us? We'll pay you." I quickly responded, "Fuck yeah! All right!" That moment set up a lot of my future history.

I had gotten sick of the Hobie team, was on Alva for a minute, and then was on Dogtown briefly as well. It was right around the time when I first whacked my hair off. I wasn't into the board that was about to come out on Dogtown, so Fausto hooked me up with Novak at Santa Cruz. Olson was the only pool rider on the SC team and a full-on punk. T.A. had blue hair and was hanging out with The Germs' contingency, and Salba was on top of his scene in the Badlands. We had the punkest team and absolutely tormented anybody who got in the way, especially the "Varibot" Variflex team.

The punk lifestyle took over our lives. We'd skate all day, go to a gig, and get hammered. We experienced many all-nighters. We would get cases of beer, and the skatepark manager would be in our pocket with the keys and the weed. We'd have chicks out there, turn the punk rock tunes up loud, and raise all hell in our own heaven. Inevitably, though, the horrible

morning sun would come up and always wreck the moment. I would sometimes wake up in the parking lot on top of a car as those Varibot geeks walked by laughing (quietly) at what a mess I was. Just the fact that they had that jock mentality would always fuel the hangover fire to do whatever you had to do. Sometimes I couldn't find both my shoes, and I'd have to borrow one half a size too small from a random kid. I took a lot of cold showers and punched myself in the face a lot to wake the fuck up. That's just the way it was. My peers and my heroes were dysfunctional misfits. So be it.

One time, after qualifying first at a Whittier contest, my board did a nosedive onto my big toe and broke it. The thing blew up like a tire, and after a couple of hours, I couldn't even walk on it. The SC guys were all staying at George Orton's house, and after we got fucking lit up all night, I was done. No contest for me. I was pissed, because Monday I was gonna have to pay a huge fine or do time for a car wreck I had gotten in a month prior.

I show up Sunday for the finals, and Fausto says, "What the fuck are you doing, man?" "My toe is broken, and I can hardly walk on it." He says, "Just try skating around without pushing, and see if it lightens up." I grabbed a board, and at first, the vibration alone was killing my whole foot, but then it kept getting more and more numb the more I rode. I never got off my board that whole day long enough for the feeling to come back. That was the ticket. I won the contest and was able to pay my fines the next day in court. It just always seemed to go like that.

Fausto always understood us and offered advice without ever actually telling us what to do. He and his wife, Gwynn, always seemed to understand our dysfunction and accepted it. Most of the time, one (if not all) of us was in the top five, with a lot of attitude and each rider acting pretty toxic. We

were all in punk bands right away, and our truck sponsor would be right there at the shows with us. The Independent crew was always at war with anybody who didn't have style, or just because. Sometimes there didn't have to be a reason, you know? The iron cross is tough, and so are our trucks. The goons have the varial, and we have the Indy air. The red, black, and white was the flag we believed in, and those are still are my colors for life. My life is "Independent," baby, and at this point, it's all gravy, no matter how it turns out. As long as I can walk, I'm gonna ride. And as long as I can talk, I'm gonna play. —*Duane Peters*

Counterclockwise from top: *The Master of Disaster copes with a hazardous frontside edger on the Combi Pool's south wall and pulls it, November 1980; Solitary frontside floater at the same spot, September 1980; Sweeping up at Colton, April 1981; A short run up didn't prevent Duane from acid-dropping the corner at the Punk Pool, January 1982.*

No other truck company can claim a trick named after it; Duane originated it and delivers the renowned Indy air to a crowd of believers at the Oasis keyhole pool, June 1980.

"Duane would walk in and just exude Duane-ness—you know what I mean? Duane had such a heavy influence." —Jeff Grosso

STAGE I

Original Release Date: July 1978
Available Sizes: 77, 88, 109, 121, 131 (Superwide), 151 (FW), 169 (MFW)
Available Colors: Silver
Features: T-Hanger Design, Solid Metal Baseplate,
Integrated Kingpin with Top Nut, Fast Action Independent Geometry

STAGE I
88 mm

STAGE II

Original Release Date: May 1979
Available Sizes: 151 (FW), 169 (MFW)
Other Available Trucks: Stage I 88, 109, 121, 131 (Superwide), 151 (FW), Roller Skate Plates
Available Colors: Silver
Features: Implemented Lower Removable Kingpin, Added "Pinch" on Baseplate for Strength,
Smoothed Additional Support Wing on Hanger

STAGE II
MFW 169 mm

Mother Fucking Wides and the Big Ten Inch

In late 1978 and early 1979, skateboard decks kept getting wider, thereby creating a need for wider trucks as well. The Independent founders, simply listening to their team riders' desires, responded with the Superwide truck, which "measured" 131 millimeters. "Indy 131s" quickly became skateboarders' truck of choice and laid the groundwork for truck widths to come.

Soon after, at a late-night dinner/business meeting/get loaded session in San Francisco, the founders agreed to create a new, even wider, truck, a decision that resulted in the 151 mm size. Although this truck size did not correspond to the actual size of the truck, the group liked that it "sounded good." Unleashing the natural marketing talents they had yet to discover in themselves, Jay and Fausto believed that making the trucks seem appealing to the skaters was more important than worrying about such an insignificant detail as the accuracy of their size. Along these lines, over the years, Independent truck sizes have ended in 1s, 6s, and 9s, more for the marketing allure of the size name than for the actual hanger width.

While the 131 mm was tagged the Superwide, the founders needed a name for the 151 as well. Stumbling into the parking lot after a dinner that included many cocktails, Fausto loudly blurted out something along the lines of, "They're fucking hot! The 131 is Superwide, so the 151 is Fucking Wide!" The others agreed; it was brilliant, and it was done.

Weeks later, prepping an ad for *Skateboarder* magazine, the founders realized that those running the mag would shut them down on the word "fuck," as they had with "fucking hot." As a result, the truck became the "FW" in print.

A few months later, creating an even wider truck became necessary, and the founders discussed "measuring" their widest product yet at 171 millimeters. But ultimately, the group of horny bastards settled on "169" instead. The next decision—to call that truck the "MFW" (Mother Fucking Wide)—was simple. And finally, when the 215 mm truck came into existence, it was known internally as "the Big Ten Inch."

Over time, the Superwide, FW, and MFW product names (the Big Ten Inch name was never used commercially) could not compete with the simpler-sounding millimeter sizes. As the Indy team riders and skateboarders across the nation began to use "131," "151," and "169" when referring to the trucks, the Superwide, FW, and MFW names were dropped.

This millimeter naming decision proved key in fostering Independent's mystique, as the size designations became a sort of secret code and a universal language for discussing the trucks. When someone said, "I ride 169s," everybody knew exactly what brand he was talking about. —*B.D.*

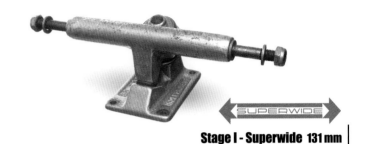

Stage I - Superwide 131 mm

Stage I - FW 151 mm

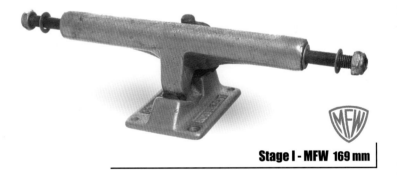

Stage I - MFW 169 mm

Standard or Metric? Neither, Really

Business, trucks, and making money weren't the Independent founders' only priorities. They also liked to party, and they indulged in all the mind-altering substances that were popular at the time. Although the Gang of Four was very focused on growing the business, when the time came to get loose at the end of the day, few people could keep up with them.

Occasionally, partying and business overlapped. One night in 1978, when the founding four were together, Jay decided that he wanted to set the sizes for the trucks. Although truck hangers then were measured in inches, Jay wanted to start using millimeters instead. He believed that doing so would be an effective marketing scheme to help set Independent trucks apart from competing brands.

His mind clearly altered, Jay grabbed a calculator and measured the truck hangers in inches, then converted them to millimeters using a formula pulled from "memory." All of his calculations were inaccurate, of course, but he insisted, "They are correct. We are done. Let's go!" None of the founders argued—they were each under the influence of their own substance of choice that evening—and the sizes were set.

True Independent diehards know that, to this day, the sizes of the hangers have never actually corresponded to their actual millimeters. Many retailers, distributors, and equipment geeks have questioned the accuracy of Independent's size scale over the years, but they have always simply been ignored. —*B.D.*

artifacts
1978-1981

I.T.C. Hard

• Left: a full set of the first Independent Truck Company stickers: red foil, black foil with "Suspension" in the cross, blue/white/red, green/yellow, yellow/orange, and the accompanying smaller versions of each. These stickers were originally packed in shrink-wrapped packs of 100, with 20 of each color.

• An original packaged set of replacement cushions (or bushings) in black. These babies were hard!

• Below: original hand-drawn bar and cross "slant" logo artwork.

• Below: Independent was the first skateboard truck to utilize cone-shaped axle washers to decrease friction between the axle nut/hanger and precision bearings. Over the years, "speed ring" became a common term for any axle washer.

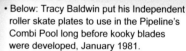

TRUCK CO.

• Below: original header-card Grindmaster packaging.

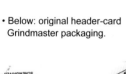

GRINDMASTER

INDEPENDENT

KEEPS TRUCKS NEW AND HANGUP FREE

SIZE
121 MM
131 MM
151 MM

NHS INC.
Jim Phillips
(408) 475-2067

5000
4"x6" FOLDED

INDEPENDENT
SPEED RINGS®
P.O. Box 1127 Capitola, CA 95010

• Below: Tracy Baldwin put his Independent roller skate plates to use in the Pipeline's Combi Pool long before kooky blades were developed, January 1981.

• Ermico produced a very limited amount of Independent roller skate plates in early 1980.

• A weathered, limited, original paper-backed "Truck Co" sticker, pre-dating production of the Stage I truck.

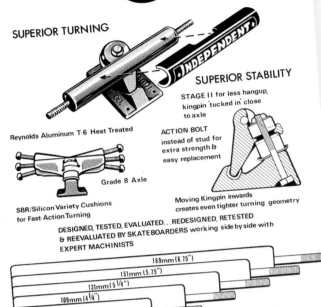

SUPERIOR TURNING

STAGE II for less hangup, kingpin 'tucked in' close to axle

Reynolds Aluminum T-6 Heat Treated

SUPERIOR STABILITY

ACTION BOLT instead of stud for extra strength & easy replacement

Grade 8 Axle

SBR/Silicon Variety Cushions for Fast-Action Turning

Moving Kingpin inwards creates even tighter turning geometry

DESIGNED, TESTED, EVALUATED...REDESIGNED, RETESTED & REEVALUATED BY SKATEBOARDERS working side by side with EXPERT MACHINISTS

169mm (6.75")
151mm (5.75")
131mm (5 1/4")
109mm (4 1/4")
88mm (3 1/2")

actual size

INDEPENDENT 88mm thru 169mm = Axle housing width

Independent Truck Company, Dept. M, P.O. Box 1127, Capitola, Ca. 95010

• Original Independent stickers, including the infamous Superwide, Bar, and Red and White Cross logos.

• Utilizing Jim Phillips' incredible illustrating talent, sales flyers like this promoted the functionality and available sizes of Independent trucks. This particular flyer shows the Stage II and its improved features.

• This Stage II logo was partially developed but never utilized.

• Below is the hand-drawn original Superwide and Bar logo artwork and color separations; Fausto boosted the Superwide logo concept from a chewing gum pack.

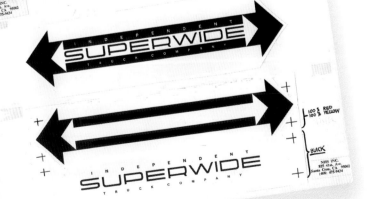

Above: *Proving his chops, Bobby Valdez pushes through a heavy grind in the Newark keyhole pool on a pair of pre-production Indy trucks. Note the conflicting stickers on his board as evidence of his recent conversion, May 1978.* Left: *Steve Olson tests the functional effectiveness of Independent's suspension truck on the transitions of Winchester's washboard. The immediate results were less than desirable: the ride was considered too soft, and a fixed-axle hanger was determined to perform better on vertical terrain, March 1978.*

Opposite page, top: *"The first time I noticed Independent Trucks; it was the Hester final at the Big O in '78, and Blackhart was doing these crazy backside roll-ins in the capsule pool. He just showed up and blew minds in a pool he had never skated before."* —Jerry "Taters" Hurtado
Bottom: *Blackhart's original (and very rare) Indy Team T-shirt.*

photo archive
1978-1981

Clockwise from above: *Wendy Gooding bounds off the coping at the Endless Wave in Oxnard, CA, August 1978; Brad Bowman and his creditable quiver of decks, August 1979; Good skatespots can be found wherever the road takes you, and Indy's riders have been turning up new discoveries since day one. Go find your own, August 1978.*

THEY'RE #★X⚡!!! HOT!

Bobby Valdez, Powerflex Team, Hester/ISA Pro Bowl #3, Newark, Ca.

AVAILABLE IN 77MM AND 88MM.

"FLASH" 4 OUT OF THE TOP 8 FINALISTS AT THE HESTER ISA PRO BOWL #3 IN NEWARK, CA, RODE INDEPENDENT TRUCKS, INCLUDING WINNER BOBBY VALDEZ AND 2ND PLACE RICK BLACKHART.

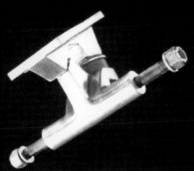

Available thru **NHS**, Inc. 825 41st. Ave, Santa Cruz, Ca. 95062 408-475-9434

Independent's second ad placement featured Bobby Valdez in front of a then–newly publicized Independent cross logo. It was the only advertisement to use the short-lived "suspension" cross logo, August 1978.

65

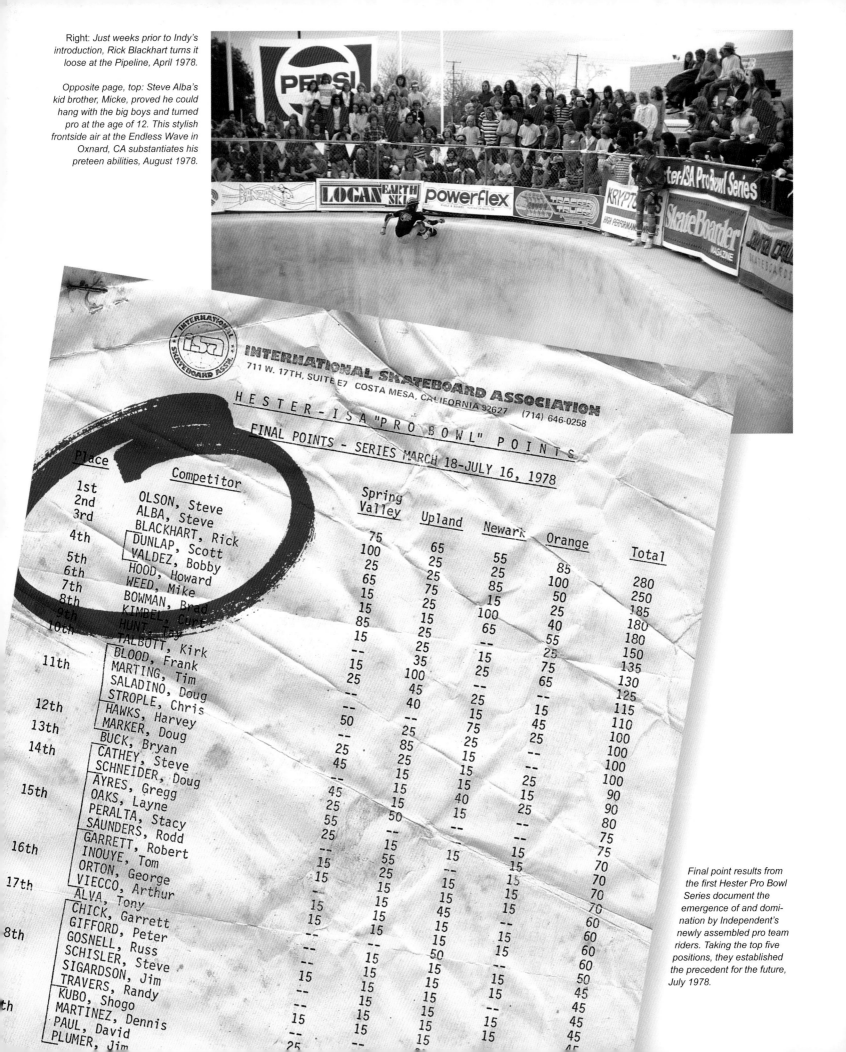

Right: *Just weeks prior to Indy's introduction, Rick Blackhart turns it loose at the Pipeline, April 1978.*

Opposite page, top: *Steve Alba's kid brother, Micke, proved he could hang with the big boys and turned pro at the age of 12. This stylish frontside air at the Endless Wave in Oxnard, CA substantiates his preteen abilities, August 1978.*

Final point results from the first Hester Pro Bowl Series document the emergence of and domination by Independent's newly assembled pro team riders. Taking the top five positions, they established the precedent for the future, July 1978.

INTERNATIONAL SKATEBOARD ASSOCIATION
711 W. 17TH, SUITE E7 COSTA MESA, CALIFORNIA 92627
(714) 646-0258

HESTER-ISA "PRO BOWL" POINTS
FINAL POINTS - SERIES MARCH 18-JULY 16, 1978

Place	Competitor	Spring Valley	Upland	Newark	Orange	Total
1st	OLSON, Steve					
2nd	ALBA, Steve					
3rd	BLACKHART, Rick					
4th	DUNLAP, Scott	75	65	55	85	280
	VALDEZ, Bobby	100	25	25	100	250
5th	HOOD, Howard	25	25	85	50	185
6th	WEED, Mike	65	75	15	25	180
7th	BOWMAN, Brad	15	25	100	40	180
8th	KIMBEL, Curt	15	15	65	55	150
9th	HUNT, Tay	85	25	—	25	135
10th	TALBOTT, Kirk	15	25	15	75	130
	BLOOD, Frank	—	35	25	65	125
11th	MARTING, Tim	15	100	—	—	115
	SALADINO, Doug	25	45	25	15	110
	STROPLE, Chris	—	40	15	45	100
12th	HAWKS, Harvey	—	—	75	25	100
13th	MARKER, Doug	50	25	25	—	100
	BUCK, Bryan	—	85	15	—	100
14th	CATHEY, Steve	25	25	15	25	90
	SCHNEIDER, Doug	45	15	15	15	90
	AYRES, Gregg	—	15	40	25	80
15th	OAKS, Layne	45	15	15	—	75
	PERALTA, Stacy	25	50	—	—	75
	SAUNDERS, Rodd	55	—	15	—	70
16th	GARRETT, Robert	25	15	15	15	70
	INOUYE, Tom	—	55	—	15	70
	ORTON, George	15	25	15	15	70
17th	VIECCO, Arthur	15	15	25	15	70
	ALVA, Tony	15	15	15	15	60
	CHICK, Garrett	15	15	45	—	60
	GIFFORD, Peter	—	15	15	15	60
8th	GOSNELL, Russ	—	—	15	15	60
	SCHISLER, Steve	—	15	50	—	60
	SIGARDSON, Jim	—	15	15	—	50
	TRAVERS, Randy	15	15	15	15	45
th	KUBO, Shogo	—	15	15	15	45
	MARTINEZ, Dennis	—	15	15	15	45
th	PAUL, David	15	15	—	15	45
	PLUMER, Jim	25	—	15	—	45

From the Other Side of the Fence

Early Observations by Dave Dominy, Founder and Creator of Tracker Trucks

"Because Jay and Rich were involved in Independent, I knew it would be significant. It caught me off guard, because they were two of my best customers; they were major skateboard distributors and central industry figures. Their combination of a team, good riders, and a good manufacturer was a winning one. All the pieces of the puzzle were in place for success."

"Novak deserves a lot of respect for the decisions he has made. If he weren't around, there would be no Independent Trucks."

"Fausto started to give trucks away at the contests, and it stung. We didn't give away a damn thing, and then those guys come in and start laying trucks on people. I think I made some mistakes in that respect, while they made some good moves, catering to the bad boys."

"They came in with Rick Blackhart and the FW trucks, and then the MFW, and then the big ads, and all of a sudden it got serious. The FW trucks were as cool as what they stood for. Tracker was clean cut, and I was thinking, 'Oh, man, that's just bad; you shouldn't do that.' In hindsight, it was actually pretty cool."

"There is no question in my mind that the truck's success stems from how it feels when you ride it. If it didn't feel good, it probably wouldn't be here today. You can throw all your engineering out the window; if it feels good, it is good." —B.D., from an interview with Dave Dominy

A legendary lineup of riders forms a luminous barrier of fabric at Newark as they ready themselves for the "Longest Carve" event. On the right, Tony Alva holds his position on a set of Trackers.

Top: *Winchester's keyhole was a well-known testing ground, and Bobby Valdez continued proving his worth with a tilted handplant reentry.* Bottom: *Teri Lawrence lets it roll on the same weekend to prevail in the women's division, September 1978.*

"Everything was pretty much a joke before Independent."

—Peter "Kiwi" Gifford

Above: *Peter "Kiwi" Gifford holds tight to a frontside drifter in the infamous egg pool at Cherry Hill, NJ, December 1978. Opposite page: Relatively unknown during the skatepark era, John Stephenson lays back on a frontside edger in the upper keyhole at Marina Del Rey Skatepark, October 1978.*

MICKIE ALBA

CASSIMUS

88 mm

109 mm

121 mm

131 mm

151 mm FW

169 mm MFW

GRINDMASTER DEVICE

AVAILABLE AT INDEPENDENT DEALERS THROUGHOUT THE WORLD

72

A full-page advertisement with Micke Alba promoting the entire size range of Independent's truck line, up to and including the FW and MFW logos and the Grindmaster Device, July 1979.

The Grindmaster Device

By Kevin J. Thatcher

Independent succeeded in reflecting rawness without accessories, so no one ever thought, "We need this or that." The Grindmaster Device was sort of a lark. Blackhart and I used to fuck around in my shop or his garage or backyard bowl, and we came up with some crazy ideas. The Grindmaster wasn't actually developed to protect the truck; the real idea, although it's sort of embarrassing to admit, was to create a slick and slippery grinding surface for rough cement, edges, and curbs.

During the first months of 1979, Tracker Copers came out. They were a package deal with a fit kit of special washers, and they cost about five bucks each, which was pretty steep in those days. The beauty of the Grindmaster was in how we made them: I'd go to the hardware store and buy a foot and a half of three-quarter-inch I.D. (inside diameter) gray PVC irrigation pipe. I just had a vision in my head that it would work. I would cut a length with a hacksaw and chop it in such a way that it snapped right onto the truck.

During the day and a half that it took to develop the Grindmaster, I was making a prototype variation and figured that I'd soften it up a bit. I didn't know you were supposed to preheat the oven and then turn it off before putting in the item. So I left the oven on, put the Grindmaster in there, went outside, and got distracted doing who knows what. I came back into the kitchen to the deadly fumes of burning PVC. It was a gnarly mess, and my mom was pissed. Kids, listen up: when the Grindmaster eventually comes back—and it will—do not cook it!

The next day, I called Fausto or Eric about taking a look at this deal. Blackhart and I drove to San Francisco and showed it to them, and it was a just a joke. It cost, like, 19 cents a foot for the material. Soon they started making them right there in the foundry, just raw, cutting them on a table saw. Some of the first ones produced were so rough and crude that they could cut your fingers if you weren't careful. The name "Grindmaster" came about through some back-and-forth ideas between Blackhart, Fausto, and me.

It was really no big deal, but the profit margin was great: I started to get royalty checks. I'd be broke, hanging at the ranch in Los Gatos (before we started Thrasher), and a check for 1,100 dollars would show up with its pay stub indicating "Grindmaster royalties." It was just righteous that that shit worked on a handshake and a promise between the founders and me, and that sums up a lot of what Independent is all about. I also have to give a nod to Jim "Bug" Martino, who later made the "Bug Master," a larger white sleeve that fit over the Grindmaster. It looked like a double-wrapped burrito on your truck.

The look of the Grindmaster era is best conveyed by the image of Salba and Scott Dunlap doing doubles in the 15-footer at the Pipeline, using Kryptos and Mother Fucking Wide trucks with perfectly clean, dark gray Grindmasters fitting wheel to wheel, tucked inside the inside wheel conicals. It was a disco look for skateboarding, but it worked.

Salba will surely testify that the coping in many skatepark bowls at that time was getting ground down to a point where there was a "coral reef" roughness developing. The Grindmaster could cut through it all.

I really don't want any credit for the Grindmaster, but I'll take all the blame.

From top: *Grindmasters in their original packaging, with an accompanying bar logo decal; Truck protection or grind enhancement? Whatever the definition, they're no longer necessary; A grindmaster in his own right, Salba puts one to use on the worn coping of the Combi Pool, September 1979.*

"I really don't want any credit, but I'll take all the blame." —Kevin J. Thatcher

73

"Independent epitomized an unruly and unkempt attitude, totally fucking rock and roll. It was outrageous, out of control, and perfect." —Brad Bowman

Superhero skater of the '70s, Brad Bowman lofts a frontside ollie above Del Mar's Skate Ranch keyhole, June 1979.

Doug "Pineapple" Saladino was the first Independent team rider to reside in the southernmost region of California. Never short for modern moves, he steps into a footplant at Oasis Skatepark in San Diego, CA, November 1979.

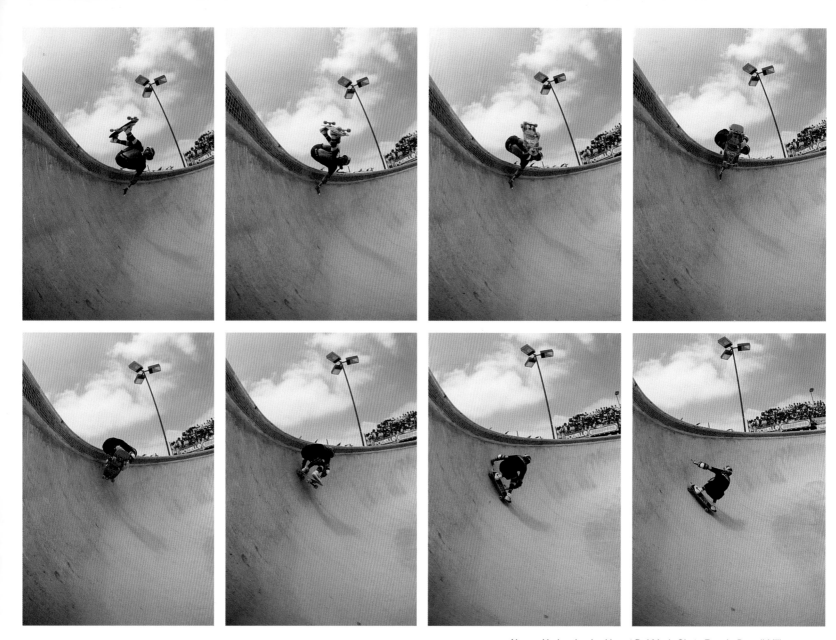

Above: *Under cloudy skies at Del Mar's Skate Ranch, Darrell Miller follows through on his inventive move, the "Miller flip," July 1979.*
Below, left: *Blackhart's well-worn and weathered Indy tee;*
Opposite: *An original collared V-neck long-sleeved shirt.*

Above, left to right: *Jay Smith's explosive layback grinds have never been replicated since he first introduced his version of them. The third frame of this sequence accurately captures his distinctive body contortion at Skate City, August 1979.*
Below right: *Two Independent cloth patches. The original bar and cross design was relieved of its duty affixed to a ballcap. The circular cross artifact is a rare bootleg, most likely from overseas. Note the misspelling of "truck."*

Top to bottom: *Skate punks in the reaches; Salba and Bowman, July 1979; Ohio "spudboys" Devo back up Olson and Bowman, August 1979; Bowman, Salba, Malba, and Bert Lamar fall in line, Boulder, CO, July 1979.*

"Independent represented NorCal skating and the statement we'd been making quietly all along: 'This shows what we're about. We're different. This is the way we do things, and we kick ass. Fuck you.'" —Scott Foss

Above: *Only a handful of skaters could jump Winchester keyhole's sizeable canyon. From the start, park local Scott Foss was one of those select few, July 1980. Below: Front and back views of Scott's rare V-neck Independent pro team shirt, which he wore in his Independent ad.*

INDEPENDENT TRUCK COMPANY

Steve Olson

Free On The Streets

Steve Olson lays low across the doubled line to uphold skateboarding's roots far from the controlled skatepark environs.
This marks the last Independent ad envisioned by Jay Shuirman. Fausto directs all ads from here on out, February 1980.

Above: *The small kid with big moves, Kevin O'Regan localized many sessions and blasted Skatepark Victoria's double bowl with frontside airs, Milpitas, CA, January 1979. Far left: Pineapple holds down the scene in Linda Vista with a new set of Stage I MFWs, September 1979. Left: Brad Bowman shreds the lip with a PVC grind at a secret Southland ditch, March 1980.*

Piloting the originator's signature deck, David "Z" Zakrzewski boosts a big ollie across a shadowy chasm at the Big O, July 1980.

Left: *A young Mike Smith helps himself to this block-busting lipslide at Marina Del Rey, April 1980.*

Below, from far left: *At a very early age, a miniature Chris Miller loads up on Indy decals and takes a bold flight above the Pipeline's Combi Pool, May 1980; Independent's triple threat, Peters, Olson, and Salba, take a break between heats during the Pro/Am Spring Nationals, Colton, CA, April 1981; Often forced to compete without a women's division, Carabeth Burnside follows through on a backside air against the dudes at Skate City, March 1981.*

Clockwise from top left: *Cruising San Francisco's Broadway strip, Andy Croft's skate car was unmistakable with its roof racks, April 1981; One of Independent's initial test pilots, Kevin Thatcher tucks a frontside air into Winchester's washboard, February 1981; Blackhart and Thatcher pack their provisions for an afternoon of skating at a secret spot, October 1980; As skateboarding declined in popularity and went underground, Tony Alva floated a subterranean frontside ollie near the mouth of the Mt. Baldy pipe, July 1981.*

SOME GET AIR, OTHERS GET HIGH!

Billy Ruff

BRAD JACKMAN

INDEPENDENT

P.O. Box 1127 Capitola, CA 95010

The parks were dying as Billy Ruff was flying in this advertisement in Thrasher *magazine, October 1981.*

Smart as Fuck, or Just Dumb Luck?

The Genius of the Jammer

By the summer of 1980 the skateboard industry was dead. Even the sales and production necessary for NHS and Ermico's basic survival had all but dried up. With no real volume to keep the machine shop operating and no cash to finance production and promotion, let alone payrolls for extremely lean staffs (NHS had dropped to four employees, and Ermico was only producing about 200 trucks weekly), the future looked bleak.

As skateboarding collapsed, many brands simply shut their doors and left suppliers high and dry with full shipping containers and trainloads of decks, wheels, and griptape. The Independent founders displayed true entrepreneurial spirit—identifying a problem and then finding a solution—and created their own salvation. They knew they had a quality truck that they had to continue distributing to the market, and through Novak's connections, they accomplished that goal by releasing a complete, ready-to-ride skateboard package called the Jammer, wrapped around a set of brand-new Independent trucks.

Kevin Thatcher recalls, "We got into Fausto's Volvo wagon to drive down to LA to skate the parks for a weekend of fun. Fausto says, 'Bring Andy Croft along.' Of course, Andy was beckoned so that we could have someone to roll joints for us and be our personal valet during the trip. On our way down I-5, Fausto mentioned to us that Novak and he had come up with this complete board setup that needed a name. During the trip, we came up with a list of names, and Fausto then drafted a final selection of the top five. We all agreed upon the name 'Jammer,' which evolved from the band The Jam, since we were just into that mode and style at the time."

Novak located unfinished 9-ply Lam-a-flex decks from a wood shop called Linderink (30 cents apiece), blemished Powell Bones and Alva Naturals from a wheel supplier called Creative Urethanes (10 cents apiece), and strips of griptape purchased by the pound, not the piece. The icing on the cake, and the only components purchased at full pop by NHS, were unassembled Independent Stage III 131 mm trucks. The trucks were delivered unassembled not only so they'd cost less but also so the NHS employees would have something to do.

Add a quick sanding of the edges of the deck, some semi-precision bearings, and a coat of black paint with a one-color Jammer screen, and put it all together at $49.95 retail. More than 70,000 units sold; many of them were shipped direct to kids, promoted and sold through ads in *Action Now* and *Thrasher* magazines.

This simple project financed the survival of Independent and NHS and generated enough consistent truck production and units for Ermico to continue developing a proper facility. This often-overlooked chain of events and simple stroke of luck/genius were major reasons why these companies managed to hang on through the lean years. They also provided a jumping-off point from which the founders could regroup and capitalize on skateboarding's rebirth in the mid- to late 1980s. —*B.D.*

"The Jammer put Independent Trucks under a generation of little kids." —Tim Piumarta

Above: *Chris Cook drops into the urban environs of San Francisco's EMB, 1980.* Right: *Jamming a frontside edge carve at Derby Park, Keith Meek grabs the rail for style points, 1981.*

Clockwise from top: *Florida's favorite son, Mike Folmer, doubles up on a frontside grab at his local ramp, 1980; Blackhart's short temper prompts explosive radicalness, November 1980; The inevitable demise of Northern California's skateparks didn't prevent diehards from getting their last licks on intact terrain. Don Fisher tailtaps the ill-fated coping at the closed Skatepark Victoria in Milpitas, Feb 1981.*

7/78 *Rick Blackhart*

8/78 *Bobby Valdez*

9/78

10/78 *Steve Olson*

11/78 *Steve Alba*

12/78 *Brad Bowman*

1/79 *Brian Buck*

2/79 *Henry Hester*

3/79 *Rick Blackhart*

4/79 *Kevin O'Regan*

5/79 *Howard Hood*

6/79 *Peter Gifford*

7/79 *Micke Alba*

8/79 *Hart & Hutson*

9/79 *Rod Saunders*

10/79 *Kevin Moore*

11/79 *Darrell Miller*

12/79 *Scott Foss*

1/80 *Doug Saladino*

2/80 *Steve Olson*

3/80 *Tony Alva*

4/80

5/80 *Duane Peters*

6/80 *Brad Bowman*

7/80 *Steve Alba*

8/80

9/80 *Mike Smith*

10/80 *Mike Folmer*

11/80

1/81 *Rick Blackhart*

2/81 *Steve Rocco*

3/81

4/81

5/81

5/81 *Micke Alba*

6/81

7/81 *Bert Lamar*

8/81 *Steve Olson*

9/81 *David Z*

10/81 *Billy Ruff*

11/81 *David Z*

12/81 *Tony Alva*

ad archive
1978-1981

Many people saw Jay Shuirman as a true visionary for his belief that skateboarding could be an industry unto itself, relying on no outside support or influence. Jay was convinced that skateboard products could be improved constantly to enhance the abilities of the skaters around him. He was wildly creative—all business and, at the same time, all heart. Sadly, he passed in October 1979 without ever witnessing the success of his many creations. His friends recall the man who shaped skateboarding in the 1970s. —*B.D.*

"I remember that Jay was ill for a while but continued to call me from his home. Jay directed the first Independent ads and came up with the concept that is now an Indy tradition: an action photo centered within a wide margin, with minimal copy and the cross logo.

"On one occasion, he called me from home and asked if I had called the magazine to tell them the ad was on its way. I told him that I had, we chatted a bit, and then I went back to work. A few days later, after having worked late into the night before, I went in feeling groggy early in the morning because another ad was running late. I ran into Rich at the top of the stairs at NHS. I held up my ad layout and began to speak. 'The ad…,' and Rich interrupted me, simply saying, 'Jay's dead.'

"I was in shock. I didn't know he was that sick. He hadn't let on that he had leukemia and was terminally ill. Rich and I were both holding back tears. I looked down at the ad and softly said that it didn't seem that important anymore. Rich told me to go on home. In my grief, I was relieved that I had obediently followed Jay's final instructions." —*Jim Phillips*

"Jay had this tenacity about everything he did; there was a physical 'presence' about him, as well as amazing intelligence. I considered him gifted—musically, physically, and intellectually. He was on a journey in his life, and we were along for the ride." —*Jimmy Hoffman*

"I remember how Jay and Rich played off each other, like a tag team. If you asked Jay for something, he'd ask if you'd asked Rich, and vice versa. In the end, they always seemed to say yes. I'll never forget Jay's big grin." —*Judi Oyama*

"Shuirman was a nutcase, intensely creative and passionate about whatever he happened to be into at that moment. He was wild eyed, scary, and dangerous—he'd stalk and attack you in the warehouse, Inspector Clouseau style—but in a moment he could become very caring, compassionate, and interested in whatever I needed to say. It was a very bad day when Rich informed us that Jay was dying." —*Tim Piumarta*

"It was Jay's vision that was the driving force behind Independent, its product, and its story. Jay got excited about everything, but he was really worked up about Independent Trucks." —*John Krisik*

"If Jay had not died, skateboarding today would be completely different; there was an energy that died along with him. Whatever type of roost there might have been, he would be the ruler of it without a fuckin' doubt. He believed that he would someday be running the skateboard industry, period. Jay was the founding father of Independent Trucks; it was just another part of the industry he planned to dominate."
—*Rick Blackhart*

"It is not length of life, but depth of life. Jay was a deep-sea diver." —*Tony Roderick*

"Jay had real compassion for the skaters, keeping me on a pro salary after my career was slowing so I could afford to launch the Hester Pro Bowl Series. He really cared about me."
—*Henry Hester*

"The whole idea of making a skateboard truck that went completely beyond the norm was such a Jay thing. He had a true 'go for it' attitude, but underneath the craziness and the bravado, you could always see a loving and caring person."
—*John Hutson*

"I remember Jay and Rich having a rotten-tomato fight in the warehouse. Jay grabbed me as a 'human shield,' with Rich yelling, 'You can't hide behind the new guy!' This was my second week at NHS. Jay had a huge smile on his face. He always made things fun and definitely interesting."
—*Steve Harding*

"You wanted to try to avoid Jay and those guys mid- to late evening, 'cuz you would pay for it the next morning."
—*Dave McIntyre*

"Jay had this detective hat, a pair of Vuarnet sunglasses, and a trench coat that he would wear; he would mysteriously show up at places, checking things out, observing, learning, asking questions. He always wanted to see and learn about what was new and happening. I remember going to a Devo concert, and there was Jay, with his hat, sunglasses, and coat, taking it all in with this huge smile, and he said enthusiastically, 'Isn't this fucking great?'" —*Mike Goldman*

"Jay was a naturally excited and vibrant person. He could have fun in a phone booth." —*Eric Swenson*

"He was a hard-ass partier and businessman … what he left behind was a philosophy of letting skaters be skaters. I'll forever miss him." —*Fausto Vitello*

"It was a huge emotional setback for me. Jay was the catalyst for the truck and all that was Independent at the time. Not a day goes by that he is not in my thoughts."
—*Richard Novak*

Jay Shuirman 1939–1979

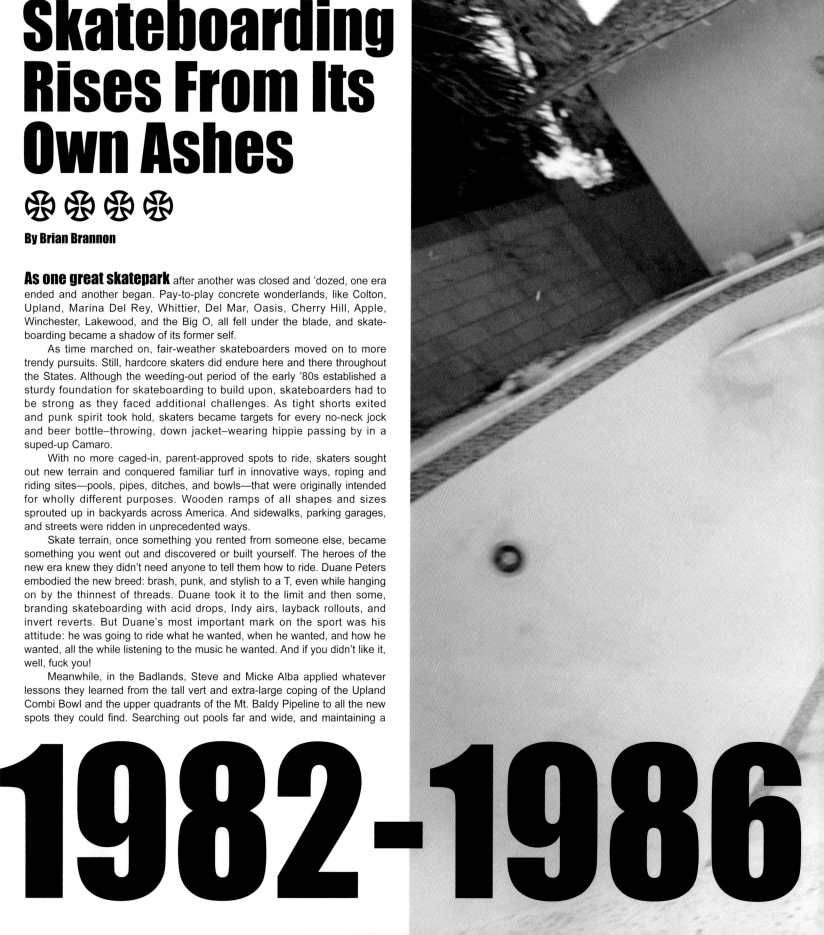

Skateboarding Rises From Its Own Ashes

✠ ✠ ✠ ✠

By Brian Brannon

As one great skatepark after another was closed and 'dozed, one era ended and another began. Pay-to-play concrete wonderlands, like Colton, Upland, Marina Del Rey, Whittier, Del Mar, Oasis, Cherry Hill, Apple, Winchester, Lakewood, and the Big O, all fell under the blade, and skateboarding became a shadow of its former self.

As time marched on, fair-weather skateboarders moved on to more trendy pursuits. Still, hardcore skaters did endure here and there throughout the States. Although the weeding-out period of the early '80s established a sturdy foundation for skateboarding to build upon, skateboarders had to be strong as they faced additional challenges. As tight shorts exited and punk spirit took hold, skaters became targets for every no-neck jock and beer bottle–throwing, down jacket–wearing hippie passing by in a suped-up Camaro.

With no more caged-in, parent-approved spots to ride, skaters sought out new terrain and conquered familiar turf in innovative ways, roping and riding sites—pools, pipes, ditches, and bowls—that were originally intended for wholly different purposes. Wooden ramps of all shapes and sizes sprouted up in backyards across America. And sidewalks, parking garages, and streets were ridden in unprecedented ways.

Skate terrain, once something you rented from someone else, became something you went out and discovered or built yourself. The heroes of the new era knew they didn't need anyone to tell them how to ride. Duane Peters embodied the new breed: brash, punk, and stylish to a T, even while hanging on by the thinnest of threads. Duane took it to the limit and then some, branding skateboarding with acid drops, Indy airs, layback rollouts, and invert reverts. But Duane's most important mark on the sport was his attitude: he was going to ride what he wanted, when he wanted, and how he wanted, all the while listening to the music he wanted. And if you didn't like it, well, fuck you!

Meanwhile, in the Badlands, Steve and Micke Alba applied whatever lessons they learned from the tall vert and extra-large coping of the Upland Combi Bowl and the upper quadrants of the Mt. Baldy Pipeline to all the new spots they could find. Searching out pools far and wide, and maintaining a

1982-1986

Guzzlin' and grindin' across a bulky lip, Jay "Alabamy" Haizlip knocks back an unruly moment at Doris' pool, July 1983.

> **"Hip-hop music? I don't understand how that goes with skateboarding at all. You gotta have guitars, man. Get in there, fuckin' skate, and turn up the music."**
>
> —Duane Peters

loose network of fellow pool dogs throughout the Southwest, Salba shaped backyard bowl-busting into an art form. Fullpipes were rare finds that skaters juiced for all they were worth; historic examples included the Glory Hole at Lake Berryessa in California and numerous top-secret Arizona specimens.

In May of 1984, *Thrasher* magazine commented that few dudes Tony Alva's age could skate as well as he did. Despite author George Orwell's overtones about the calendar year, Alva Skateboards was going strong. Throughout Southern California, TA was dominating backyard pool sessions, including the legendary Doris' in Rossmoor and other hush-hush treasures. An up-and-coming young pup named Christian Hosoi, from the wilds of Marina Del Rey Skatepark, was also riding for Alva at that time.

In years to follow, Christ-brah would make a name for himself as a master blaster of humongous airs and stylish slash-dog moves. Hosoi eventually started his own skate company and went on to rule the world with sky-high McTwists, the trick that distinguished the top three finishers from all the other participants in any contest of the era. Hosoi's main rival was a skinny kid named Tony Hawk. Whereas Hosoi was a power skater from the surf/skate school, going big and carving hard, Hawk's tricks—deemed "circus moves" by some people—were more technical and multi-syllabic. Whether Hosoi or Hawk won a contest often depended on who was judging that day.

Some skaters couldn't have their way with a handy supply of cement wonders; for them, backyard ramps became the terrain of choice. Almost without fail, skaters who capitalized daily on access to vertical halfpipes carried the deepest trick bags. California, with its abundant pools and pipes, was the land of milk and honey, but vert ramps were what enabled skaters in the rest of the country to ply their trade.

While ramps, pipes, and pools were getting their fair share of abuse, skaters in the mid-'80s continued taking it to the streets. Parking blocks, parked cars, and everything in between became fodder for coping-inspired moves like curb grinds, slappies, street plants, and rail slides. The first street style contest took place in San Francisco's Golden Gate Park in 1983, and local boy Tommy Guerrero used his speed and pop to take home the gold. Countless others honed their own styles on the street; young Turks like Mark Gonzales and Natas Kaupas foreshadowed moves that would become standard more than a decade later.

Meanwhile, bands of skaters were unleashing a new strain of music, known as skate rock, to provide the soundtrack for a thousand sessions. From Austin, Texas, by way of Pflugerville Ditch, The Big Boys laid down fun and funk. In Arizona, JFA showed the world what too much surf-style skating in the middle of the desert would do to your brain. In Oxnard, California, Aggression released *Intense Energy*, as Agent Orange splattered *Blood Stains* and surf music to fuel skaters everywhere. Minor Threat used DC hardcore to convey the idea that drugs, alcohol, and smoke are nothing to get excited over. Other noteworthy skate bands from that time include Code of Honor, Los Olvidados, Free Beer, McRad, The Faction, Die Kreuzen, Suicidal Tendencies, Drunk Injuns, Gang Green, and Ill Repute.

Confidence was critical for the stunt wood pirates, whether they were hitting ten o'clock in a secret desert pipe, grinding away an afternoon in a backyard pool, or assaulting the environs of Street Town, USA. And through it all, Independent remained the truck of choice and the standard-bearer for hardcore skateboarders everywhere.

From top: Thrasher *magazine's inaugural Skate Rock weekend had JFA's Michael Cornelius providing the bassline of aggression at San Francisco's Tool and Die, May 1983; Sporting an original Indy lid, Randy Katen lights up, September 1982; Christian Hosoi styles with toe control at the Hell Hole, February 1985.*

Clockwise from above: *The Big Boys' Tim Kerr shows that he's got soul at the Skate Rock show at the On Broadway, June 1984; With the skate industry down in the dumps, John Lucero gives rise to a tail tap in Whittier's keyhole, February 1982; Steve Caballero and Gavin O'Brien tune into The Faction's set at the Tool and Die, May 1983.*

*Christian lofts a stylish lien air above the Mile High Ramp,
Tahoe City, CA, July 1984.*

christian HOSOI ✛ ✛ ✛ ✛

"They have always let me be me — not only as a team rider but as a part of the Indy family." —Christian Hosoi

Christian Hosoi epitomizes finesse, fluidity, grace, style, confidence, influence, and true friendship. He has always been of a rare caliber. The first time I met Hosoi—or "Big Daddy," or "Holmes," or even "Christ"—we became friends.

Holmes and I first met in our barrio, Venice, California, which for us was the Mecca of skateboarding. Somebody had once described Christian to me as a chick with muscles, but I couldn't see it. He was the first person to put me on a plane, the first person to take me out of the country, the first person to show me Hollywood, Hawaii, Japan, and Brazil, and the first person to introduce me to Independent Truck Company and my buddy Joey Tershay. Traveling with Christian was always an adventure. No matter what country, demo, contest, or club he went to, he made people feel like they shouldn't miss it.

Christian's essence, especially the friendship part, is most apparent in the photographs we made together. With his finesse, he made shit look so easy that he had you thinking you could do the same, even though you never could. With his fluidity, he made skateboarding look like his destiny. With his grace, he stood out from the crowd like the true Hollywood rock star that he was. With his style, Christian not only set trends with his skateboarding but also customized his attire to suit himself; soon, he'd have the people around him wearing stuff they usually wouldn't. With his confidence, he achieved things no one else could. And with his influence, he set goals and benchmarks that we all continue striving to accomplish.

Christian is responsible for my involvement with the skateboarding industry and Independent. In the lifestyle we've chosen to lead, Christ and Indy go hand in hand. —*Cesario "Block" Montaño*

Christian got his first skateboard in Hawaii, with Chicago trucks and Cadillac wheels, when he was five years old. I went down to a Local Motion, where we had been making surfboards, and I made a skateboard for Christian. It was a '70s surf-style board, based on the Jerry Lopez Lightning Bolt model. It looked like a mini gun. Skateboards never had a tail then, but I made the tail on this board go down to the ground so Christian would have a brake system. It was a downhill jam with the nose going up. One day Christian was riding it backwards, and he said, "That brake thing isn't happening, but the nose kicktail is working." I told Christian to hang onto that board, as it was one of the first kicktails, but a Chicano stole it right off the front porch in L.A. From that point on, Christian never let his board out of his sight.

Eighth grade was gnarly for Christian. He was going to a school in L.A., right on Robertson and the freeway, where a lot of gang shit was happening. Every day, the gangs rousted Christian. I worried that one day it would go too far, but Christian had his system down. He would wear two watches—a cheap one on his wrist and a good one in his shoe—and he would keep three dollars in his pocket and 20 dollars in his shoe. The gangs would take off his watch and his pocket cash, but they never stole his skateboard because it didn't interest them. Eventually, though, even Christian's strategy got too gnarly. So one day I asked him, "What do you want to do?" And he said, "Just skate." After that, he took on skating full time 'cause the school thing was just too dangerous.

We used to go to Brazil and do street demos. It was crazy; homeless kids would chase our car down the street. Christian gravitated more to the homeless kids in Brazil than to the skaters, 'cause they were tough little

101

"The first time Independent really struck me was when I saw Christian Hosoi for the first time. His whole setup and style really made Independent stand out. That's what made me a believer." —Danny Way

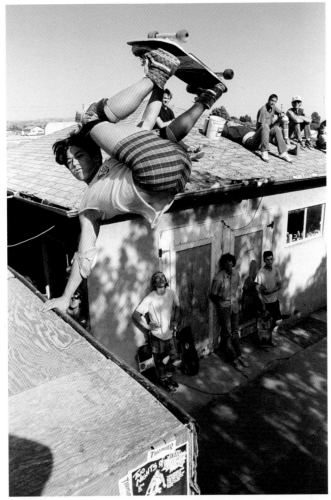

Clockwise from top left: Only Christian could bring style to such an ugly trick as the layback air, Joe's ramp, May 1983; Christ air pose in front of Rio De Janeiro's Christo Redentor, 1989; Kicking it at home in his closet full of flair, July 1991; Christ makes eye contact on a casual layback at Del Mar's keyhole, December 1986.

kids, and they wanted it. They would watch our car for two dollars while we went to a restaurant, and we'd say, "Two dollars? No problem!" If you did not pay them, though, they would throw mud or take the hubs. One night Christian bought extra dinners to give to the homeless kids. He just wanted to stoke 'em out. —Ivan Hosoi

During the hang time that he got in those backside airs, when he would kick his foot out and just hang, Christian found a lot of opportunities to experiment in the air. Eventually, that led to his rocket airs, his Christ Airs, and his McTwists. Hosoi had the power, doing high-speed rock and roll slides the length of the pool. It was an inspiration to see him taking skateboarding to a top-notch level. He was the king of the world.

Even after a contest was over and every other pro was gone, Christian would still be in the parking lot, spending time with the kids, giving them stickers, signing autographs, talking to them, and being cool. He was always the last guy to leave the party or the session.

Christian was consistently generous, too. He always had lots of people hanging around him, and even if he was having dinner with 10 people, he'd pick up the bill. He never cared, because he was with his homies, and he was making money, so he wanted to care of the crew. —Dave Duncan

I'm at the skatepark with my friends, and I look over and see this girl skating, and she's fucking ripping, you know what I mean? This girl's doing lien airs to tail, just ripping the pool, and I go to my friend, "Dude, who's that chick?" and he goes, "Dude, that ain't a chick; that's fucking Christian Hosoi!" He ripped, man. I just sat there and watched Christian kill it.

We were in Brazil for about two weeks while Christian did this thing for Global TV. Everywhere we went, every restaurant, every nightclub, everybody knew Christian. The little neighborhood kids out front of the house said, "Hey, you're the guy on TV!" Chicks were always coming up to Christian, too. We moved to the front of every line and got red-carpet treatment for two weeks. That's just how he was living; he could go into anyone's neighborhood and take over the town, be more of a local than

nightclub people or regulars at the skatespot. Christian was always down for the adventure of it. He wanted to tune in and plug into the town more than anybody: where's the backyard ramps, the pools, the party, the cool people to hang out with?

At the Long Beach trade show one year, Christian had a rental car, and we were going to Hollywood to party. We had a whole car with five or six dudes; Cooksy and all the boys were there. We were driving as Christian tried to pass a joint to the guy in the back seat. As he was looking over his shoulder, the road turned. Christian didn't see it, and he pulled the steering wheel, and the car went up on two wheels on its side, cruising, and then boom! It slammed to the ground so hard that we got two flat tires. We all had to skate two miles back to Long Beach, and Christian, all calm, called the rental car company and said, "Hey, your car's got flat tires. Go get it." That's just how we were living back then.

In the late '80s, skateboarders were getting rock star status, crowds, hype, travel, and money. Christian helped raise skateboarding to that level. He had the charisma and character and attitude that represented the true spirit of skateboarding: go as high as you can, and live life to the fullest.

Christian was also the ultimate showman. He'd be at a contest, waiting for his run to start, and the music would play for 15 seconds while the judges waited for his run to start. Meanwhile, he'd be dancing, adjusting his shit, looking around, and making sure his five shirts hanging off him were showing the right logos. Then, all of a sudden, he'd drop in and win the contest, just blow doors. The place would erupt.

When I asked him about the money, I said, "Christian, what if it all ends? You should at least buy a house." He got mad and said, "Eddie, I'm going to spend all this money, but we're going to make it again. You don't make it the first time; you lose it. It's the second time around that you keep it."
—Eddie Reategui

Above, left to right: *Christian put style in street competitions and drops a banger at the Capitol Burnout event in Sacramento, May 1986; Blazing the late-afternoon skies in Christ air fashion at Patty's perfect ramp, Arizona, 1988; This rocket air at Skilley's ramp became an icon for an era of new moves, July 1987.*

tommy GUERRERO ✠ ✠ ✠ ✠

"With the whole NorCal thing, you couldn't not ride Indy. You would probably get beat up." —Tommy Guerrero

No discussion of street skating's roots is complete without mentioning Tommy Guerrero. From a very young age, Tommy learned to adapt to and navigate San Francisco on his skateboard. Although he frequently visited Bay Area skateparks, pools, ditches, and backyard ramps as a teenager, the streets provided the most accessible terrain for TG and his crew of friends.

As the curtain fell on the '70s and the skateparks of that era, San Francisco's burgeoning punk rock movement caught the attention of Tommy, his older brother, Tony, and several of their cohorts, and skateboarding became primarily a method of transportation for them. They occupied themselves instead with musical instruments, playing gigs in bands called Jerry Kids, Revenge, and Free Beer. San Francisco's thriving and renowned punk scene became the passion of and creative outlet for the young gun and his associates. They also supported many touring bands of the era, including Black Flag, Social Distortion, Circle Jerks, Personality Crisis, Toxic Reasons, The Adolescents, and D.O.A.

Thanks to the bootstrapped efforts of *Thrasher* magazine, skating was soon reborn. Backyard ramps and street skating images appeared monthly on the newsprint pages, and the magazine's D.I.Y. attitude breathed new direction in life into a bleak industry. As a second-wave skate scene developed in San Francisco, Tommy eventually returned to skateboarding and found a new playground on the city's streets.

As a relatively unknown and unsponsored amateur, TG won the first-ever pro/am street-style contest in San Francisco's Golden Gate Park. TG stunned many of the competing pros that day with his smooth, innovative style, but because he was an amateur, he was forbidden to collect cash winnings. But shortly thereafter, through his involvement with Independent

Truck Company, Tommy met Stacy Peralta, who signed him on as a member of Powell Peralta's elite Bones Brigade.

Tommy won the first contest he entered as a professional and subsequently became the first pro skater to endorse a signature-model skateboard marketed exclusively for street skating. These significant moments occurred at a time when vertical skating dominated the pages of the magazines, although street skating was fast emerging as the preferred means of conquering uncharted terrain. Tommy greatly influenced and facilitated the spread of the revolutionary street movement. In the era of street plants, TG pioneered ollie grabs (and soon after, kickflip grabs) off launch ramps.

Tommy traveled incessantly with the Bones Brigade on rigorous demo tours, participating in competitions and making appearances that inspired countless kids around the world. He also devoted long hours of filming and skating to production of Peralta's cult classic *The Search for Animal Chin*. His fame led him to a few small acting roles on the big screen in *Police Academy 4* and *Gleaming the Cube*. But even as Tommy achieved iconic status, he remained grounded and loyal to the streets of his hometown.

In 1990, Tommy parted ways with Powell Peralta to start his own skate company, Real Skateboards, with his friend and fellow pro skater Jim Thiebaud. Over the years, Real has absorbed a number of other premium skate brands. All the while, Tommy has fostered his creative spirit through a variety of successful musical endeavors: with several bands, collaborative projects, solo recordings, and a few international tours to support his craft, TG's plate is always full. Of course, he still finds time to grind, and no matter what, it's with the distinctive style that's made him a legend.

—*Bryce Kanights*

*Tommy's self-styled and boundless approach to skating
left an indelible mark on a new generation of youth.
Jump ramp–assisted wall ride, January 1987.*

"When the parks closed, we had nowhere to go, so we skated whatever we could find. If there was a pool down the block, you skated the pool. If there was a fullpipe at the beach, you skated the fullpipe. If there was a jump ramp in the middle of a schoolyard, you skated that. It was never a conscious decision; we just skated."

—Tommy Guerrero

This page, clockwise from top: *TG boosts a frigid air during a spur-of-the-moment skate jam in Berkeley, CA, November 1986; TG owns the streets, December 1987; Drainage ditch ollie in Pleasanton, CA, 1981.*

Opposite page, clockwise from top right: *Tightly tucked lien air at the Summit Ramp, June 1982; Tommy makes sensible use of modern architecture, April 1987; Snatching up a slob air at Shrewgy's short-lived back-yard haven, February 1984; TG pioneered ollies into assorted grabs off jump ramps, and this face-high stalefish was dialed long before it became routine, December 1987.*

steve CABALLERO ✠✠✠✠

Left to right: *Chin Ramp channel crossing, 1987; Strumming chords at home, 1988; Afternoon bench carve at China Banks, 1987.*

"Even the name is strong. Independent is what skateboarding represents." —Steve Caballero

Steve Caballero will go down in history as one of the greatest skateboarders of all time. His offerings to our pastime will far outlast our generation's days on Earth. He created a legacy based on achievements, but he did it by doing what he does best: having fun.

As a wee lad growing up in San Jose, Stevie excelled in all the activities he participated in. His approach was to silently study, in great detail, the technique of others who were doing what he wanted to do, and then dive in with a confidence most of us could only pray for.

Between Eddie Elguera and Tony Hawk, there was a time when Stevie was skateboarding's master. He invented his own tricks, won all the vertical contests, traveled the world, started a band, helped invent street skating, and even made his own 'zine. At the start of this period of his life, he was riding for Tracker Trucks, whose sales and team loyalty paralleled Indy's at the time. In Stevie's own hometown, an Indy stronghold, his friends hassled him daily about his choice of trucks. I know this because I was one of the main offenders. When he finally agreed to switch to Indys, with Fausto himself sitting in Steve's living room, he shocked the skateboard world. Stevie was skateboarding's Wayne Gretzky, and he left Tracker for Independent. Steve Caballero was an Indy rider!

Coke vs. Pepsi, Apple vs. Microsoft, Raiders vs. 49ers … these rivalries have nothing on the Independent vs. Tracker battle that raged in the '80s. Two different companies, two different magazines, two completely different cultures. Tracker promoted finesse; Indy, brute strength. Steve's old sponsor never really recovered from the switch, while Independent went on to become not only a skateboarding legend, but also a worldwide icon with more brand recognition than the entire industry combined.

That's what my pal Stevie did. —*Gavin O'Brien*

Caballero remembers the early days of Independent's rebirth and the influence of *Thrasher* magazine:

"It was all about grinding and turning. They wanted skaters who skated, period. Nothing flashy; just full-core, hardcore gnar. Independent would make these special contest shirts only for Independent riders. I just thought it was awesome. No other companies would do that, and the tees were not available to the public. It made us a part of an elite team.

"I don't think Fausto gets enough credit for getting out on the road with us and endorsing the backyard ramp events that basically created an industry. When skateboarding died in the early '80s, his support really helped the sport, and so did *Thrasher,* with Fausto, Mofo, and KT running the magazine. They were not afraid to finance and promote new things, but it wasn't always about promoting Independent—it was about skateboarding first." —*B.D., from an interview with Steve Caballero*

Many of his peers believe Cab boasts the best frontside inverts in the business. He rocks one at full tilt before a crowd of landlocked onlookers at the Midwest Melee 2 in Lincoln, NE, September 1984.

Clockwise from top: *With his rear truck facing forward, Cab tweaks a distant backside tailbone beyond the hinges, June 1987; Straight-armed tuck-knee invert on his chopped backyard ramp, October 1987; Steve pounds the pavement with a contorted jump ramp launch at the Capitol Burnout, May 1986.*

"When Caballero got on Indy, it was a big deal. After he switched teams, everyone who liked progress came over to Indy, too." —Mark Gonzales

Steve leaps into a face-high frontside boneless at Joe's ramp, May 1984.

"For Caballero, riding for Indy was kind of his passage into manhood: leaving Tracker and the little kid thing and going where the men played. It was so cool to watch it all go down."

—Jeff Grosso

STAGE III

Original Release Date: October 1983
Available Sizes: 99 (Streetstyle), 131 (Superwide), 159 (FW), 169 (MFW), 215 (Big 10 Inch)
Other Available Trucks: Stage I 88, 121
Available Colors: Silver
Features: Smoothed Pivot on Hanger, Beefed-Up Support Wing on Hanger

**STAGE III
MFW 169 mm**

**STAGE III
99 mm Streetstyle Truck**

STAGE IV

Original Release Date: March 1986
Available Sizes: 159 (FW), 169 (MFW), 215 (Big 10 Inch)
Available Colors: Silver, Black
Features: Further Smoothed Pivot on Hanger, Smoothed and Balanced Support Wing

**STAGE IV
215 mm**

STAGE V

Original Release Date: October 1986
Available Sizes: 149, 159 (FW), 169 (MFW)
Other Trucks Available: Stage I 101, Stage IV 215
Available Colors: Silver, Blue, Maroon, Gold, Purple, Green, and Black
Features: New 149 Size, All-New Lightweight and Durable Hollow-Body Hanger

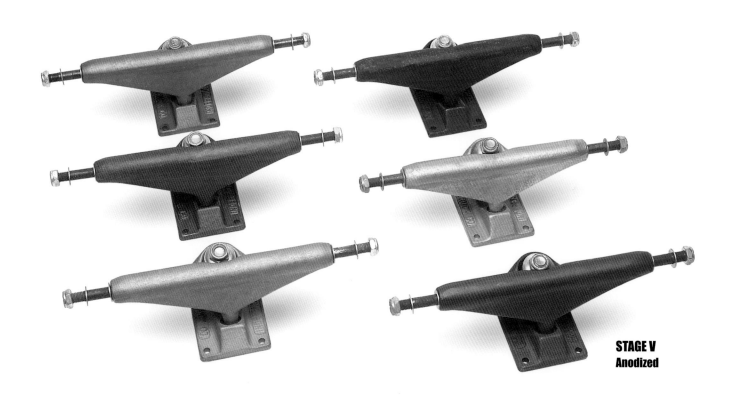

STAGE V
Anodized

The Hollow Body
by Steve Caballero

In 1986, we were on a Powell-Peralta tour with Mike McGill, driving around the country in a station wagon. Tours back then were so low budget that we had a launch ramp on top of a station wagon; that was our demo every time we went to a skate shop.

We realized, "Indy hasn't come out with something new in a while. Let's make a new truck for them." We had paint pens that we used to draw on our griptape with. We used a paint pen for the axle and an actual Indy baseplate, and we molded the hanger with sculpting clay we bought at a store. We just started molding this truck, and it actually started turning out to be pretty good.

McGill got wind of it and got all jealous, and he said, "I'm gonna make a truck for Tracker." He was in the front seat driving, and Lance and I were in the back seat designing this truck. We kept hiding it from him. The more we hid it, the more he wanted to see it. Our idea for the truck was simple: we wanted to reduce its weight and add some strength at the same time. It was the first truck with a hollow design where you could see the exposed axle underneath.

We finished the truck after the tour and took it to Fausto. The ironic thing was we had no idea that he and Eric were already working on a new hollow truck that was similar to ours. Fausto was stoked and gave us a nice bonus for the work we had done.

By 1986, I had some prototype Stage V Hollow Bodies that I took to the Vancouver '86 Expo. I did really well in that contest, and after my run, I slam-dunked my board from the top of the ramp to the flat bottom. All these kids from the bleachers started running after it. Hundreds of kids thought I had done a board toss, and a big fight ensued. I ended up getting on the mic and saying, "Hey, I need that board back. Those are experimental Independent trucks." We got the board back, but I got fined 500 dollars—half my winnings—by the contest organizers for causing a riot.

artifacts
1982-1986

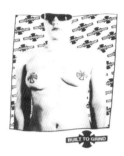

• An ultra-rare Built to Grind team T-shirt from the controversial ad that pissed off quite a few people.

NEW 99mm 'STREETSTYLE' TRUCK

PROVEN GEOMETRY

SUPERIOR INDEPENDENT STABILITY

INCREDIBLY LIGHT WEIGHT – STILL INDEPENDENT TOUGH

356 Aluminum T-6 Heat Treated, w/ Grade 8 Axle

New Hanger Design – Light Weight

Created to meet the demanding needs of the Freestyle Skateboarder!

99mm Width fits most of today's Freestyle decks.

Designed, Tested, Evaluated & Redesigned, Retested and Reevaluated by the best Professional & Amateur Freestylists working side by side with Expert Machinists!

Independent Truck Co, Dept. M, P.O. Box 1127, Capitola, Ca. 95010

• This logo concept is an interesting play on the rounded cross but was never further developed.

• "Designed, Tested, Evaluated, & Redesigned…." This sales flyer promoted the new 99 mm Streetstyle truck, actually a freestyle truck. It featured an extremely trimmed-down hanger and pivot with grade-8 steel axles.

• Hard-to-find, hand-painted Built to Grind canvas banners like this one could be seen at contests during the era and were usually stolen by the time the contest was over.

114

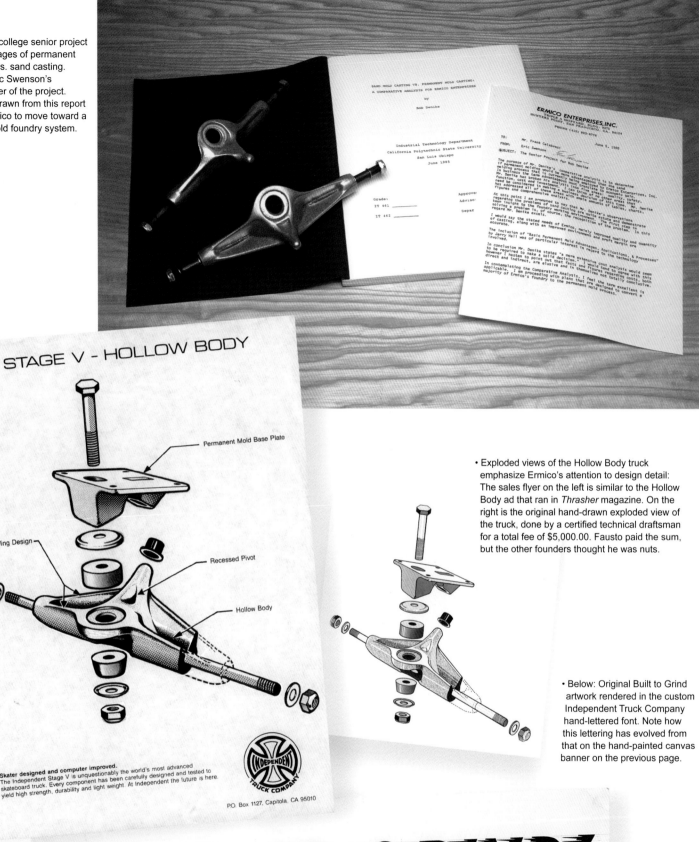

• Bob Denike's college senior project on the advantages of permanent mold casting vs. sand casting. Included is Eric Swenson's evaluation letter of the project. Conclusions drawn from this report prompted Ermico to move toward a permanent mold foundry system.

STAGE V - HOLLOW BODY

Permanent Mold Base Plate

Double Wing Design

Recessed Pivot

Hollow Body

Skater designed and computer improved.
The Independent Stage V is unquestionably the world's most advanced skateboard truck. Every component has been carefully designed and tested to yield high strength, durability and light weight. At Independent the future is here.

P.O. Box 1127, Capitola, CA 95010

INDEPENDENT TRUCK COMPANY

• Exploded views of the Hollow Body truck emphasize Ermico's attention to design detail: The sales flyer on the left is similar to the Hollow Body ad that ran in *Thrasher* magazine. On the right is the original hand-drawn exploded view of the truck, done by a certified technical draftsman for a total fee of $5,000.00. Fausto paid the sum, but the other founders thought he was nuts.

• Below: Original Built to Grind artwork rendered in the custom Independent Truck Company hand-lettered font. Note how this lettering has evolved from that on the hand-painted canvas banner on the previous page.

BUILT TO GRIND!

A Spark of Life in a No-Direction Time

By Mörizen Foche

One day in late 1977, while I was learning to ride vert at a place called the Los Altos Pool in NorCal, Kevin Thatcher, Steve Weston, and a guy named Rick Blackhart showed up and tore the place apart. This Blackhart guy, they called him "Rubberman," and aside from being exactly that, he was fearless. His personal temperament complemented his aggressive skateboarding style perfectly; he was very cocky, and he ruled the pool in every sense. I hadn't seen anything like it in my skateboarding experience or in the media. But I know now that in this balance of attitude and reckless, yet calculated, abandon lay the answer to my own questions about the direction skateboarding needed to take.

The original Independent team riders—Blackhart, Olson, Salba, and Peters— epitomized my perception of skateboarders: they had cool, combative, devil-may-care demeanors, incredible riding styles, and innovation and charisma. They were tangible, but they lived and acted in ways most people only dreamed of. Their enduring attachment to the Indy phenomenon over these 25 years proves that we were right to hitch a ride on the Independent locomotive.

One particular pivotal event for me that molded the Indy spirit and the trajectory of skateboarding happened one evening at a Clash show at San Francisco's Kezar Pavilion during the weekend of a Hester Series comp at Winchester. Skaters were there in force: Olson, Salba, Bowman, TA, Duane, Mark Baker, Kiwi, Blackhart, Thatcher, Tim Lockfeld, Fly, and a few founding members of the Jaks Team. We congregated around Fausto and his lovely wife, Gwynn, who was wearing open-toed high heels, on the dance floor. We arrived in time for the end of the opening act, Dead Kennedys, and saw Jello Biafra dive into the crowd, only to emerge stark naked and wearing only one shoe. When the following act, The Cramps, came on, we watched the crowd do "the pogo," which was vogue at the time. Throughout the set, the lot of us were roughhousing, throwing each other around and banging into people. Bonding in a new way with comrades we had never met before, we just did what we felt

like doing, because of the Indy connection, because of skateboarding, and because we were hearing a new kind of music that tied it all together.

Momentarily, the crowd pulled back to allow some room for our energy. One of us would grab another by the arm and begin spinning him around fast. When one of us took a tumble, it was dog-pile time. By the time The Clash took the stage, we were amped and transformed into a formidable band of brothers. On the first crashing note, the crowd started pogoing like crazy. When that happened, we looked at each other and understood silently that this pogoing stuff was already passé, that it had to end right away, and that we were going to be the ones to do it.

Spontaneously, we charged the crowd from behind, pushing them forward until there was no more room. Then we climbed on top of them and crawled across their heads until a few people, out of heads, found themselves standing on the stage without a plan. By the time the security beef recovered from their initial shock, we had all scrambled back and joined the rest of the group. We picked up where we had left off with our dervish-like activity and amplified it tenfold, thus creating the very first slamdancing pit. Gwynn got her toes stomped on, but she forgave us.

People who attended the Hester contest the first day knew that skateboarding had taken a distinct off-road turn into a more hardcore realm. Months earlier, at the Newark Hester Series contest, Independent had made its debut as a force to be reckoned with. At Winchester, the cult of the Independent brotherhood was unveiled. Unplanned, it occurred because it just had to happen. New blood had been injected into our veins, and it gave us new life and a new sense of belonging.

The first time I met some of the men responsible for those magical turning devices was at Winchester Skatepark, in the back area by the infamous keyhole pool. Rich Novak, Fausto Vitello, Eric Swenson, and Jay Shuirman were there. I only have one distinct memory of Jay—he passed away before we could spend much time together—and that was of when I was hanging out by the fence, watching Kiwi skate. Jay walked up with a Sharpie in one hand and grabbed my face with the other and drew a line across each lens of my sunglasses. Dumbfounded, I watched as he walked away laughing. I had never seen such agro, forward behavior. I was astounded; I was mesmerized.

Rich Novak wasn't as in your face as his business partners and seemed to prefer remaining in the background, but he taught me one of my most important life lessons. One day in 1981, when I'd been working at *Thrasher* magazine for just a few months, Novak was in the office for a meeting with Fausto and Swenson about how to keep skateboarding alive. I

Clockwise from above left: A pint-sized and unknown Tommy Guerrero surprised all comers at the first-ever street skating contest, April 1983; Christ on deck, February 1983; Malba traverses the channel at the Great Desert Ramp Battle, February 1983; The flyer announcing the first S.F. Street Style contest, April 1983.

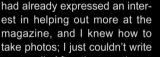

It's time to go to work!" The guy has always been strictly business, ready to rock at six in the morning. I thought if he could do it, I could do it. But I still cannot reach the level of commitment to the cause that Swenson possessed then and still possesses today. It is that commitment that fuels Independent trucks.

had already expressed an interest in helping out more at the magazine, and I knew how to take photos; I just couldn't write very well. After the meeting ended, I was informed that Mr. Novak was gonna give me a little talking to. He sat me down and started telling me about learning how to write, and before long, he convinced me that it was pretty simple. He also gave me a paperback book called *Fear and Loathing in Las Vegas,* by Hunter S. Thompson. I'd never heard of this magical book or the author, and I had no idea what to expect. "Now, Mofo," he said, "read this book, and I swear to you, when you're through, you'll know how to write." I was wondering what in the fuck this guy was talking about, but I said okay.

I read the book as fast as I could, and then I was eager to test it out. After a contest in Morro Bay, I drank as much booze as I could, came back home, took some acid, and started typing my story on a very shitty typewriter, hunting and pecking psychedelically. Around three in the morning, I called Fausto and told him, "Dude, I'm actually writing, and my fingers won't stop, and there's demons flying out of the walls, and the fucking floor has turned to liquid!" By the time the sun came up, I'd filled 20 typewritten pages with words until my fingers couldn't push the keys anymore, and then I wrote another 10 pages by hand. Fucking Novak. He taught me that I could do anything if I wanted to.

I was roommates with Eric Swenson for a couple of years. We lived in an apartment that had a huge deck with an incredible view of the San Francisco skyline. In the evenings we'd go to bars, where he introduced me to the wonders of cocktails. We started off with screwdrivers, then moved on to greyhounds, and after that, there was no way to remember. I just knew I'd taken a giant leap away from cheap beer. By the time we crawled back into the pad after each of these excursions, we were obliterated. But early each weekday morning, no matter how hard the drinking had been the night before, Swenson would kick me in the head. "Get the fuck up, Moped.

Fausto Vitello—or "V," as some of us called him—has always been the enigmatic personality behind Independent's image and the idea man, the soul, the leader of the Independent cult. When he faced a mountainous challenge, he chose not to go around it or over it, but to charge through it. He led, and continues to lead, by aggressive example, inspiring everyone around him to join him in hot pursuit of sometimes insane adventures. Fausto and Eric also took care of their people. They were always available whenever any of their guys was in a bind, whether because of a family emergency, a personal tragedy, being in jail, or just plain needing a good drug connection.

Much of the skate world portrays the Independent founders as vicious, cutthroat dictators. What these critics fail to realize is that their views obscure the reality that the founders are merely employing assertive business practices and possess the foresight to initiate radical change. Without these ideals and the vision to achieve them, Independent Truck Company would never have survived, and skateboarding as we know it today would never have had a platform to grow from. We have these men to thank that we even have a skate industry and a worldwide Indy community. I was nothing more than a big fan, but Indy was invigorating, a spark of life in a no-direction time. And after all this time, it still energizes the souls of those of us who were there at the beginning.

Clockwise from above left: *Billy Ruff hucks a frontside invert at the Clown Ramp, Dallas, TX, November 1984; A legend in the making, June 1983; Steve Steadham at Joe's Ramp, January 1984; Unnoticed by a clique of freestylers, Mofo banks on Del Mar's reservoir, September 1983; Captain Olson navigates the channel at the Mountain Manor, December 1984; Lance Mountain stays connected and maintains his skate regimen on the road, October 1986.*

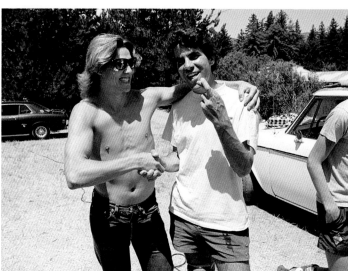

Opposite, clockwise from top: *Getting down on his home turf, Micke Alba tosses up an Indy air at the Pipeline, June 1983; Young dudes Blackhart and Denike keep their eyes on the prize at the Summit V ramp contest, June 1982; Cliff Coleman hangs through a laid-back slide on the winding hillside streets of Berkeley, CA, December 1981.*

Above: *Taking the initial leap, Christian Hosoi bomb-drops into the history books at Cab's backyard ramp, January 1983.* Below: *A pair of worn and well served Indy bushings.*

photo archive
1982-1986

Above: *Rob Roskopp commits to a lapover grind at the Dolphin Pool in Ben Lomond, CA, November 1983. Below: By the early '80s, Independent's Grindmasters were produced in three colors, each imprinted with a string of logos.*

Opposite page, clockwise from top: *With 169s affixed to a handmade plank, Tommy Kay lets it fly above the Ramp Ranch II, Atlanta, GA, July 1983; Boards, beers, and bros in Sacramento, CA, June 1982; The always-explosive Tony Alva turns up the heat across Doris' loveseat, July 1983.*

"Indy riders have fuckin' pride man, straight out. Doesn't matter what board, wheels or bearings you have; if you have a set of Indy trucks, your shit is 100 percent." —Tony Alva

STOP SKATE HARASSMENT

Post Everywhere

This public service announcement is brought to you by **INDEPENDENT**

Independent Co-Founder Eric Swenson serves his duty in this public service announcement, October 1982.

Clockwise from top left: *Mountain and Steadham, hungry for action. November 1984; Spidey and his street shred, May 1984; Randy Katen lays it down in the Sacto heat. April 1984; Tommy Guerrero boosts a*

Above: *As parks closed, skaters took to the backyards with their skills and thrills. Corey O'Brien sails a mute air in front of a fenced-in crowd in Milpitas, CA, October 1983. Below right and opposite lower left: A pairing of two Independent T-shirts.*

Opposite page, clockwise from top: *In limited yard space, Chris Cook pops an ollie at Luis' ramp in San Francisco, May 1983; Randy Katen taps the edge at Tahoe City's Mile High Ramp, 1984; A collected and unjaded Christian Hosoi floats a fashionable ollie at the Capitola Classic, September 1984.*

"Independent Trucks are for core, time-proven skaters. There are some of you who should not ride them. You know who you are!"

—Randy Katen

"One of the raddest things in my skateboarding career was getting my first yellow Independent paycheck. It was like, 'I have arrived!'"

—Jeff Grosso

Above: *Cab and Mountain double up on plaid shirts and knee pads and barrel through a parking garage in Dallas, TX, December 1983.* Left: *Flirting with the bridge of death, Bryce Kanights steps up to a boneless one at Joe's ramp, November 1983.* Opposite page: *Jeff Grosso reaches toward the exit on this eggplant across the Mile High Ramp's channel, July 1984.*

Above: *Mondo pummels a plywood lip in Playa Del Rey, CA, January 1984.*
Below, from left: *Doubles in trouble, Keith Meek and Steve Caballero roll the dice at a street style event in San Francisco, May 1984; San Jose's infamous Montegue Banks hosted many late night sessions; Spidey follows through on a slappy 5-0 grind, September 1985; Scott Foss steadies an Andrecht on a lengthy loveseat, Saratoga, CA, March 1985.*

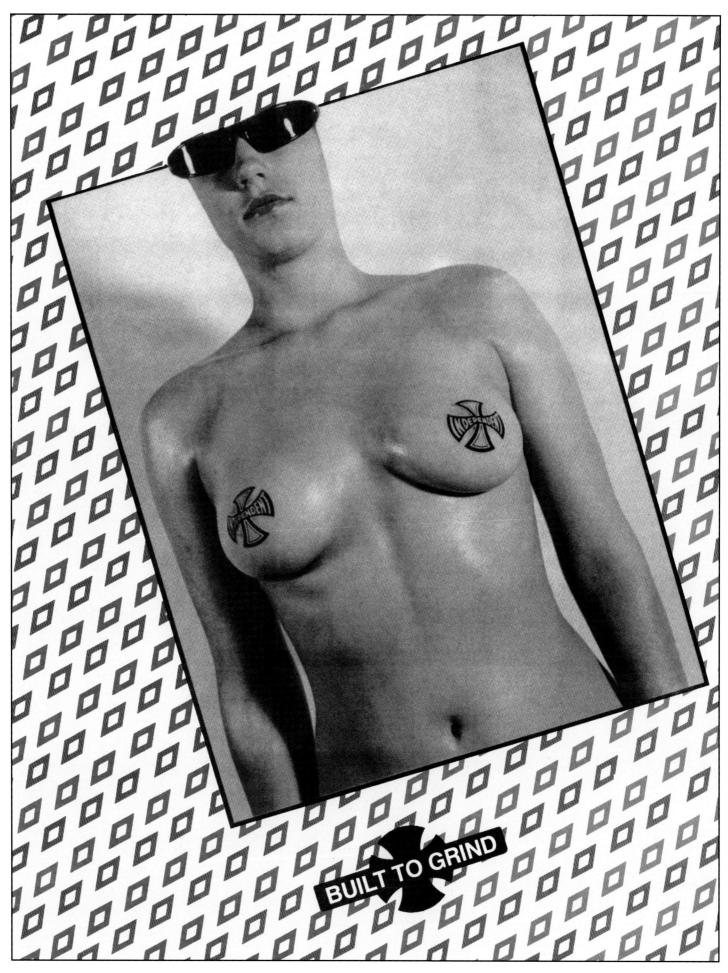

This advertisement prompted other manufacturers in the industry to start up their own skateboarding publication in an effort to counter the edginess of Thrasher *magazine and its collective founders and followers, February 1983.*

The dynamic duo of Caballero and Mountain double up
in the Pipeline's steep and deep Combi Pool, June 1984.

Right: *At the site of the first-ever ramp jam, Joe Lopes steps into a bean-to-tail (AKA a "Joeless One"), March 1985.*
Below: *Joe's original Indy team sweatshirt.*

Right: *Tommy's older brother, Tony Guerrero, proves that style runs deep in the family with this pivotal two-wheeled slide in San Francisco.*

131

Top: *Alan Losi frontside lipslide at Del Mar, August 1984.* Bottom, left to right: *Hugh "Bod" Boyle serves up a boneless one at London's Southbank, 1985; Demo dog Roskopp pushes a frontside invert before a crowd in Modesto, CA, March 1986; One of the first to do so, Mike Archimedes hits a frontside carve over a bench at SF's China Banks, December 1985.*

Opposite page: *Vertical veteran Micke Alba adds the right amount of seasoning to an eggplant at San Francisco's HP Ramp, October 1985.*

Clockwise from left: *Owen Nieder straight-arms a layback air at Del Mar, January 1985; Not far from the Nike Missile Site SF-88, Tommy Guerrero launches under the afternoon sun at Fort Cronkite, April 1986; English freestylist Graham "Mac" McEacheran hucks a sadplant at San Francisco's Dish, March 1986.*

STEVE STEADHAM

INDEPENDENT   INDEPENDENT

Box 1127, Capitola, CA 95010

A C.R.Stecyk III–designed ad pays homage to skateboarding's timeless soundtrack with Steve Steadham's embellished boom box, January 1984.

Mike Smith finds a new line and acid drops the hip of the Pipeline's Combi Pool, June 1985.

Clockwise from top left: *Sweeping up the channel of the Mush Ramp, Greg Aguilar was one of San Jose's hottest rising talents, May 1986; As the lights go on, Texas' John Gibson jumps into king-sized frontside boneless one at Del Mar, August 1985; Jay Adams' surf influence becomes apparent at Del Mar's large banked reservoir, April 1984; Lance Mountain sets the Mile High Massacre ablaze with a scorching lien to tail, Tahoe City, CA, June 1985.*

Clockwise from top left: *No matter where his skating took him, the globetrotting Christian Hosoi never ran out of lovelies, Virginia Beach, VA, June 1986; A self-made statement of the times, Lance shows support with his original T-shirt design, 1985; Trucks are meant to be grinded: a pair of well-used archetypes, May 1986; Limited-edition team shirt, 1985.*

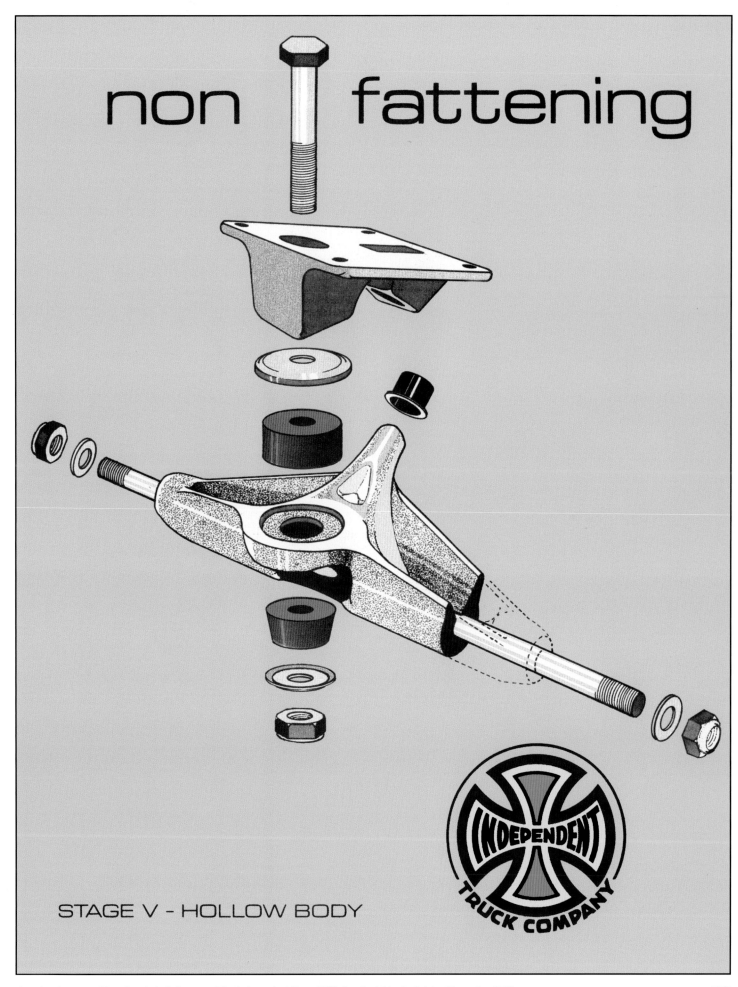

An advertisement with an "exploded" diagram of the Independent Stage V "Hollow Body" truck, October/November 1986.

1/82

1/82

3/82 *Doug Saladino*

4/82 *Bob Denike*

5/82 & 6/82 *Street Scott*

7/82 *Chris Baucom*

8/82 *Henry Rollins*

9/82 *Rodney Mullen*

10/82

11/82 *Randy Katen*

12/82

1/83

2/83

3/83 *Christian Hosoi*

4/83 *Jay Adams*

5/83

6/83 *John Gibson*

7/83 *Steve Caballero*

8/83 *Micke Alba*

9/83 *Rob Roskopp*

10/83

11/83 *Lance Mountain*

12/83

1/84 *Steve Steadham*

2/84 *Steve Olson*

3/84

4/84 *Rodney Mullen*

5/84 *Steve Caballero*

6/84 *Mike Smith*

7/84 *Brian Brannon*

Thrasher magazine ▶

8/84

9/84

10/84

11/84 *Monty Nolder*

12/84 *Steve Steadham*

1/85

2/85 *Lance Mountain*

3/85 *Steve Caballero*

4/85 *Tommy Guerrero*

5/85 *Claus Grabke*

6/85

7/85 *Billy Ruff*

8/85 *Craig Johnson*

9/85 *Christian Hosoi*

10/85 *Jonny Kopp*

11/85

12/85 *Micke Alba*

1/86 *Rob Roskopp*

2/86 *Tony Guerrero*

3/86 *Billy Ruff*

4/86 *Tommy Guerrero*

5/86 *Jeff Grosso*

6/86 *Lance Mountain*

7/86 *Christian Hosoi*

8/86 *Steve Caballero*

9/86 *Rodney Mullen*

10/86 & 11/86

12/86 *Eric Dressen*

ad archive
1982-1986

No More Heroes ✠ ✠ ✠ ✠

By John Dettman-Lytle

During the '80s, vert ruled, and the air wars were on. Hosoi and Caballero, who both blasted past the 10-foot mark during that decade, proved that when style, experience, speed, and control were combined, the only thing left to do was to go higher … and hold on. At contests, judges hotly debated whether precise technical skating or more crowd-pleasing air shows should take precedence. Was style king? Where did height or difficulty fit in? Tricks were becoming so diverse that any maneuver might never be the same twice, depending on who was doing it, which foot was coming off the board, and how many individual tricks it incorporated.

Skateboarding was evolving at a feverish pace; it had established a legitimate competition circuit, which was actually starting to get television coverage, and it was finally receiving the widespread accolades it deserved. Even the untrained eye could appreciate how challenging it was for skaters to adapt to and pull off the increasingly difficult moves of the day. Even if you had the gift, you still had to skate long and hard just to keep up. If you were shaky, you were likely to get hurt and become more famous for your slams than for your skating. Good style and control helped keep skaters in one piece and allowed the core vert establishment to continue laying it on the line for itself, for the crowd, and for future generations to come.

Meanwhile, however, an increasing population of skaters without adequate facilities for vertical skateboarding would soon emerge out of the gutter to steal most of the spotlight, showcasing what the streets now had to offer. In growing numbers, skaters could no longer refuse readily rideable terrain. Tranny or no tranny, skaters will be skaters, and they discovered quickly that handplants could easily be street plants. Jump ramps came and went, saving any remaining

ankles for handrails and stairs. And the skateboarding media, always looking out for the next big trend, pointed their cameras downtown.

A "no more heroes" approach took over as more skaters everywhere realized the true potential of their immediate surroundings. Trucks once grinded only in pools and ramps found their abuse elsewhere. And although a true skater's board is never a dust collector, no matter what shape it is, for the first time, street-specific decks were designed. Groms everywhere snatched them up, along with 149s and 159s instead of the wider 169s.

Even with this sudden surge in street skating, you can't fight the facts. Remaining pockets of energy that identify with no trend are always percolating. Try saying "vert is dead" to the diehard vert riders who didn't give a damn (and still don't) if they were a day late and a dollar short. Or try telling that to the dedicated few who only cared about skating with friends or alone and continued building ramps in suburban backyards.

When mini-ramps became popular in '88, they established a middle ground where street and vert skaters could meet and keep skateboarding progressing. Mini-ramps in the six-foot range were the breeding ground for much modern technical, lip-oriented vert skating. Skateboarding was spreading deep into uncharted, and previously unimaginable, global territory. Seeing skaters execute tricks that most people had only dreamed about became commonplace. If you could visualize something, it could be done, sometimes even by the end of the session.

By 1990, many pros felt compelled to leave their respective sponsors and start their own companies, although no one dared invade the truck market, which Independent had cornered. Some skater-owned companies made perfect sense and did well with core values. Others were in all corners of the ring, scheming over whose image they were going to taint or copy next. Spoof renditions of nearly every popular logo on the planet introduced the term "cease and desist" to skateboarding's vocabulary. In the deck realm, the industry's political climate grew heated, as plummeting sales led to some underhanded marketing techniques. Real skaters took note, made choices and rolled forward, a tad more jaded but remaining ahead of the pack. Credited for their innovation, for inspiring a host of other activities, and for dictating youth clothing fashions worldwide, skaters still weren't content to call it a day. They went right on chiseling their influences in stone, ushering in the dawn of a new decade.

Meanwhile, back at the lab, Independent was busy manufacturing trucks the entire time.

Jump ramps gave rise to various street skating tactics in the '80s. Eric Dressen makes good use of one to clear a yellow post in Venice, CA, August 1986.

1987-1990

From left: *The Grossman mugs it up, 1987; Kicking out the jams at San Francisco's HP ramp, July 1985; A priceless portrait of skate politics, Virginia Beach, June 1986.*

jeff GROSSO

"Trucks are supposed to be mean; you grind them. They're the meanest part of the skateboard." —Jeff Grosso

Jeff Grosso started skating at age 12 at Desert Surf Skatepark in Las Vegas. But it was when his family relocated to Southern California, where he discovered Skate City Skatepark in Whittier, that his love affair with skateboarding really began. His parents, taking advantage of the ultimate kiddie daycare, would drop him off at the skatepark every morning and pick him up there every night. The arrangement was mutually beneficial; Jeff skated tirelessly all day, stopping only long enough to grab a Big Gulp and a candy bar.

Although tile and coping abounded in Jeff's second home, simple carving and grinding couldn't satisfy him. Jeff wanted more. He wanted to tail drop, so I taught him. He wanted to roll out, so I showed him. But then he wanted to roll in, and I couldn't do it. I wasn't gonna let this little kid know that, though, so I pulled it first try and told him I did it all the time. While I pushed him, he pushed me. He had style and skill from the start, and I knew he was gonna be one of the best.

Young Jeff backed up my prediction between 1981 and 1983 in ASPO and CASL, the Little Leagues of amateur skateboarding. Consistent and progressive, he mastered every modern skate trick as quickly as he had that first tail drop. Jeff won almost every contest he entered, and people noticed; soon, he was opening boxes of free skateboards that the UPS man, a.k.a. "The Happy Man," dropped off on his front porch. It couldn't get any better. Or could it? Jeff thought so.

By 1984, Jeff—now called "Mothra"—was riding for Powell Peralta. He beat out the best skaters at the Del Mar nationals and became the number-one amateur in the world, kicking off a virtually unbeatable two-year reign. But Jeff still wanted more: he wanted a shot at the pros

The Bones Brigade said no, but his friends said go. That was all the encouragement Jeff needed; he jumped ship and turned pro, never to look back. Skating higher, faster, longer, and louder than ever, the brat turned up the heat in the pro ranks and brought his "right here, right now" attitude to the big show.

By 1987, the parks of the past were long gone. Plywood and Masonite had replaced concrete; steel pipe had replaced pool coping; and skateboarding was making a triumphant return. The Grossman was at the top of the crop with huge airs and an even huger attitude. He wanted more, and more he got—more money and more fame.

Jeff made contests more exciting with his distinctive rock 'n' roll flair, which extended far beyond competition; skate all day and party all night was the only way to be. But it couldn't last forever; the days got shorter, and the nights grew longer, and by the end of the '80s, the money was gone, and so was Jeff's drive. He was high and dry and addicted to the night.

In 1990, vert skating was dead, and street skating was much more than a dork session on a curb. The new generation didn't care, and the vert dinosaurs couldn't relate. But The Grossman stayed in the game by helping the upstart company Black Label, selling product and shipping orders. In the off hours, still skating, the dark side still chasing him, Jeff battled sobriety and his personal demons. And he finally caught himself and put the past behind him. Clean and sober from here on out. I'm proud of that kid. He's my little brother. He may fall, but he always gets back up. And through all his ups and downs, one fact remains: The Grossman rides 169s.

—John Lucero

El Jeffe reclines into a punk-infused layback roll-out at Holmes' ramp, Hollywood, CA, October 1989.

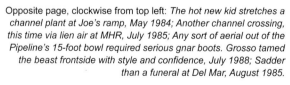

Opposite page, clockwise from top left: *The hot new kid stretches a channel plant at Joe's ramp, May 1984; Another channel crossing, this time via lien air at MHR, July 1985; Any sort of aerial out of the Pipeline's 15-foot bowl required serious gnar boots. Grosso tamed the beast frontside with style and confidence, July 1988; Sadder than a funeral at Del Mar, August 1985.*

Clockwise from top left: *Psychedelic frontal rock at the Pipeline, February 1989; Grosso gets a leg up on Sean Penn with this mighty Madonna at the Del Mar Fairgounds, February 1990; Sharing a carefree moment with longtime pal John Lucero in Toronto, May 1988; Extended to the toes with a backside boneless at Del Mar, May 1986.*

"It was pretty much the only thing that remained constant with us. Our wheels changed on a weekly basis, and our boards changed on a daily basis, but riding Indys always remained the same." —Jeff Grosso

DRESSEN ✠ ✠ ✠ ✠

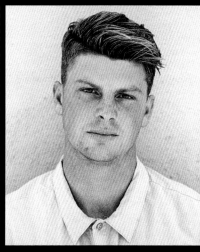

"Being hardcore is Independent. It's a lifestyle, and everyone adopted it." —Eric Dressen

Like a quiet storm, Eric Dressen will arrive in the midst of a fully brewed skate session and, without warning, fire up the scene with his skating abilities. In fact, he will fuck shit up; his wheels will smoke, the coping will burn, and cheers will fill the area.

During the late '70s, Eric, the pup from Dogtown, was surrounded and influenced by heavyweights and skate veterans from the Santa Monica and Venice regions. When the Z-Boys were in their prime, terrorizing the streets, backyard pools, and reservoirs—and, later on, the legendary skateparks—their antics directly inspired and guided Eric at an early age. At age 10, Eric was featured in *Skateboarder* magazine in a much-coveted "Who's Hot" profile; at age 12, he turned pro. Perhaps by chance, little Dressen got his first set of Indys from Duane Peters in the parking lot of the Big O Skatepark.

Nearly a decade later, Eric ruled a growing industry with his powerful brand of skating and became the back-to-back World Street Champion in 1987 and 1988. As a second-generation Dogtowner, he affected a nation of kids with his raw yet stylish, contributions to skateboarding. In fact, Dressen invented the salad grind, although not many people know that because he's never been one to spray about it. Despite the acknowledgments and awards he's received since he began turning heads as a small tyke, Eric prefers to just skate and grind hard in a session with his friends.

Eric expresses himself through his skateboarding, and he does so loudly, with speed and experience. But off the board, he's a quiet, mild-mannered guy who doesn't want to be the center of attention. He's just that modest and pure. He's down for skateboarding at its core level without catering to its mass-marketed hoopla. Eric is a skater at heart and can tear into any terrain you put in front of him with confidence and control. Just give him the opportunity, and it's guaranteed that you'll be sitting down, watching in awe. —*Bryce Kanights*

Eric makes a sick trick all the better with this textbook-styled backside crailtap at Gonzo's pool, May 1989.

Clockwise from above: *On his way to victory with a toe-tweaked frontside nosebone above Big Surf's chlorine-dusted wave pool, Phoenix, AZ, November 1987; Warming up the afternoon with frontside crail scraper at SF's China Banks, February 1988; Little Eric D. packs power in his kick and thrusts double overhead above an alignment of five-and-a-half-foot trannies, Powell warehouse, November 1989; Digging up abandoned art, or just another headstand? Louisville, KY, June 1988.*

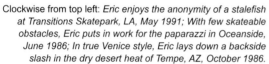

Clockwise from top left: *Eric enjoys the anonymity of a stalefish at Transitions Skatepark, LA, May 1991; With few skateable obstacles, Eric puts in work for the paparazzi in Oceanside, June 1986; In true Venice style, Eric lays down a backside slash in the dry desert heat of Tempe, AZ, October 1986.*

"I love my trucks. My trucks are my prized possessions. I don't let my friends stand on my boards 'cause I have them adjusted just right. If someone steps on my board, it fucks it up. It's one of my superstitions." —Eric Dressen

ray
BARBEE ✪ ✪ ✪ ✪

"It's the turning; this truck reacts with me." — Ray Barbee

The summer before he entered seventh grade, Ray Barbee's friend Danny received a Variflex skateboard for his birthday. As the two boys cruised down the street, Ray on his bike and Danny on his new board, Ray got jealous. Danny was just having way more fun. Fortunately, Danny remembered that his father had been a skateboarder, and in his garage he found an old Sims Wood Kick with ACS trucks for Ray to ride.

When the duo returned to school, they bragged to other kids about rolling around all summer and ended up finding a crew of six or seven other kids who had done the same. Ray would end up spending the majority of his youth with this group. They built a quarter pipe, and then another quarter pipe, and then added some flat bottom, until the ramp eventually became an eight-foot-high, 24-foot-wide halfpipe.

With no lights to skate the ramp after dark, Ray and his friends spent their evenings trying tricks they'd learned on the ramp on curbs, in driveways, and in the street. With so much uncharted terrain to explore, and by reading a few magazine articles about street skaters like Gonz, Natas, and Tommy Guerrero, Ray's interest in street skating grew and grew.

Ray became close friends with a skater named Robert Torres around the time that magazines began expanding their street skating coverage. Because local ramps had disappeared or were too far away, Ray and Robert realized that they needed to start traveling to Sacramento, where the skate scene was really starting to bustle. There, Ray found inspiration in people like Ricky Windsor and Randy Smith, who were leading the charge of modern street skating.

Ray never thought about getting sponsored, but Robert started talking about it more and more as both friends improved. Robert repeatedly called companies to ask for endorsement, and eventually, he and Ray became sort of a package deal. On one fateful day, they met Tony Alva at a contest, and he approached Ray to ask if he would be interested in riding for Alva.

As an Alva team rider, Ray had frequent travel opportunities, especially to Southern California, where he skated in Venice and the surrounding areas. He eventually met a young Chet Thomas and Tommy Guerrero at a few contests, and they both mentioned Ray's talent to Stacy Peralta. Weeks later, at a contest in Carson, California, Stacy saw Ray skate and asked him to ride for Powell Peralta.

Ray broke new ground in street skating with his technique and grace in Powell videos. His street skating wasn't about embellishing freestyle tricks; he would flow down the street, using the terrain and creating lines. His style set the standard for video parts for a decade to follow.

As the story goes, Ray was riding for another truck company at the time, even though he'd ridden Independent Trucks for most of his days on a skateboard. But when he tried skating the hills and avenues of San Francisco with Tommy and Julien Stranger, his trucks prevented him from making the turns his friends could as they cut and carved in and out of driveways and corners. He broke down and had to pick up his board and run just to keep up. The next day he saw Fausto and asked if he could ride for Independent.

Ray has been leading, not chasing, ever since. He is dedicated to contributing to skateboarding and having a long run. While others have dropped off, Ray has never left; he's been here the whole time, smiling and flowing, becoming a part of skateboarding's history. —*Lance Mountain*

*Ray stands tall on this tasteful
frontside noseslide in San Francisco,
June 1996.*

"I've ridden other trucks before. I felt like I was always tightening them, loosening them, trying to figure out bushings, trying to get that feel I was used to with Indys. After that, I just had to ride Indys." —Ray Barbee

Clockwise from above: *Flirting with disaster becomes a midnight delight when the property owner is away for the weekend, October 2002; The ever-smooth Ray grinds a lip without a transition to get there, Berkeley, CA, 1998; Over the bars with a 180 heelflip in Spain, 2001.*

Clockwise from top: Ray keeps it gnarly with a 50-50 on a waist-high ramp accessory in San Francisco, 1997; Shopping for music makers in Memphis with Tommy Guerrero, October 2002; Frontside heelflip above the tightly transitioned jai alai courts in Phoenix, October 1995.

"Once you get into skateboarding, you never see things the same."

—Ray Barbee

STAGE VI

Original Release Date: November 1991
Available Sizes: 149, 159, 169
Other Trucks Available: Stage I 101, Stage IV 215
Available Colors: Silver, Blue, Maroon, Gold, Purple, Green, and Black
Features: Reduced Material on Top of Hanger

**STAGE VI
169 mm**

• This never-used distorted version of the oval cross logo was created by moving the logo on a Xerox copier. Behind and to the left are the color separations for the oval cross decal.

• An oval cross decal from 1990. Below: Original paste-up board for an NHS catalog page promoting the Stage V Hollow Body and other Independent Truck accessories.

INDEPENDENT TRUCKS AND ACCESSORIES

Skater designed and computer improved. The Independent Stage V is unquestionably the worlds most advanced skateboard truck. Each component has been carefully designed and tested to yield high strength, durability and light weight. At Independent the future is here.

INDEPENDENT TRUCKS SIZE GUIDELINES

TRUCK	DECK TYPE	DECK WIDTH
101mm Freestyle silver, blk/red/blu/purp	Freestyle	7.0"
149mm - V silver/blk/red/blu/purp	Mini or street	9.0" - 9.75"
159mm - V silver/blk/red/blu/purp	Mini, street, ramp	9.75" - 10.5"
169mm - V silver/blk/red/blu/purp	Ramp	10.0" - 11.0"
215mm, silver	Ramp or sailboard	11.0" - +

INDEPENDENT TRUCK ACCESSORIES
"Snap" urethane truck suspension cushions, Independent "Speed-Ring" axle washers, Independent "Grindmasters", Independent pivot cups and assorted hardware. Also available is an extensive line of decals, painter's caps, t-shirts and sweatshirts.

STAGE V   HOLLOW BODY

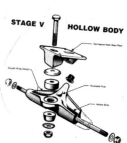

• A "stretched" oval cross sticker; one of many experimental variations on the Independent logo that went down over the years.

artifacts
1987-1990

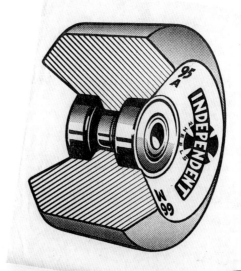

• Don't get too excited; this wheel graphic was developed strictly for trademarking purposes.

• Original hand-cut color separations for the Bar and Cross logo.

• The short-lived Indy *Team 'Zine* featured team rider profiles and humorous stories.

• One of the better-known, but ultra-rare, team T-shirts made famous by numerous team riders. Mark Gonzales wore a short-sleeved version in his first Independent ad, "The Only Choice."

• Many authorized dealer decals have come and gone over the years. This one, seen along with its original artwork, ran throughout the '80s and was reissued in 2003.

Opposite: *Legendary Z-Boy Jay Adams lets loose on the lip in Venice Beach, CA, 1987.* Above: *Speed and confidence award Mike Youssefpour a distant touchdown on this early-release backside 360 spinner at Donner Ski Ranch, August 1987.* Right: *A classic team tee that speaks the truth.*

photo archive
1987-1990

SUPERIOR IN THE STREETS

INDEPENDENT TRUCK COMPANY

P.O. Box 1127
Capitola, CA
95101

C.R. STECYK III

ERIC DRESSEN

Advertisement featuring back-to-back World Street Champion Eric Dressen, March 1989.

Under chilly autumn skies, Andy Howell cracks a crailtap in the deep southern suburbs of Atlanta, November 1988.

Left: *Danny Sargent's rear truck; weeks of non-compulsory slappys, hurricanes, Smith grinds, feebles, and general abuse led to the altruistic result of one hammered Stage V. Opposite page: Danny Sargent hangs tight to a frontside air at the Grim ramp, giving his trucks a short respite from usual wear on the city's streets, May 1989.*

Above: *Cooley's ramp gives Doug Smith a frontside ollie drift, June 1990. Below: Steve Caballero and Lance Mountain resist the silhouetted remains of a skate session in Milan, Italy, July 1988.*

I'D
RATHER
FIGHT
THAN
SWITCH

Christian Hosoi in an advertisement endorsing what most skaters have long known as "Indy Pride," November 1989.

Clockwise from top left: *A moment of reflection with Jay Adams, February 1989; In the midst of a secret Phoenix pipe mission, Steve Olson sets it loose on a frontside thruster, August 1988; Reggie Barnes steadies a handstand on his trucks in Münster, Germany, 1987.* Lower right: *An Indy bracelet handmade from a baseplate.*

"What about just fucking rolling? Do you skateboard for fun, or do you skateboard so you can get high, get paid, and go and get filmed and see yourself in the magazine?" —Steve Olson

"The bottom line is that there's a sense of pride in that name and logo. Independent represents everything skating is about: sessioning hardcore, without a care what others think." —Tom Knox

Clockwise from top left: *Chris Robison unleashes a backside disaster at the Prime Evil Pool in Chino, CA, May 1990; With miles of style, Mike Carroll snaps up a lien at Studio 43, July 1990; Permission pools are a rare find, and TSOL's Ron Emory lays in his legal licks at the Sign-In Bowl, July 1989; San Jose's Kennedy warehouse hosted many ramp locals during its short history. Jeff Kendall was one of them. Kicked-out tailbone toward the rafters, San Jose, CA, April 1989.*

The teenage phenomenon widely known as Jovontae Turner hangs tough on a huge ollie to axle stall during a small and secretive backyard ramp session in San Francisco, August 1989.

Declaration of Independent. Free to be, July 1990.

Clockwise from top left: Jeremy Henderson cruises through a G-turn between the North and South Towers of the World Trade Center, NYC, June 1989; The streets of San Francisco get a dose of northwestern talent in the form of Shawn Martin, April 1989; Second-generation Dogtowner Scott Oster heats up the San Fernando Valley with a backside slash over the steps, June 1990; Hot shoe at the Phoenix Am finals; Thomas Taylor takes to the lip with an Indy jar, December 1988.

Clockwise from above: *Lance Mountain corners a tucked frontside deep in the environs of East Los Angeles, October 1988; San Francisco's one and only Pierre "P Double" Benitomako footplants from a seaside ledge, July 1989; The original purveyor of pranks and mischief, Ricky Winsor leans back in the clutch of a liquid-courage layback grinder, May 1989.*

*Sergie Ventura tweaks a
straight-legged backside
air high in the clouds
above Virginia Beach's
Mt. Trashmore ramp,
October 1989.*

Rare team shirts from the late '80s, clockwise from top right: *The only team design with the INDY spelling; A modified "Fucking Hot" tee; FW cross design; The Blaze tee.*

Just prior to the death of vertical skateboarding, Mike Youseffpour kept the gnar factor in check with this lien air at the Northwest Qualifiers, Redding, CA, November 1989.

High in the attic of the Pipeline's tube, there is no way Screaming Lord Salba can actually see his board on this ridiculous frontside thruster, May 1989.

"Salba charges—and he charges hard. You get around someone like that, and it just rubs off on you." —Jeff Grosso

Scarred for Life
Independent's Indelible Icon

These photos represent just a few examples of the many people who have gone so far as to tattoo the Independent logo on their bodies for life. Over the years, Independent's cross logo has become a cultural totem of sorts, representing individuality and pride in self-sufficiency. Be yourself. Be Independent. —K.W.

Top, left to right:
Jeff Grosso, Ted Shred, Mikey Whaley.
Middle, left to right:
Barrett "Chicken" Deck, Joey Tershay, Dustin Dollin, Dave Richardson.
Bottom, left to right:
Darren Navarrette, Gus Colonel, unknown.

"There's no other skate company that has inspired nearly as many tattoos on people as Indy." —Colin McKay

Clockwise from top left: *John Lucero levitates a king-sized frontside ollie at San Jose's Kennedy warehouse, April 1989; Craig Johnson rises above the shadows of Mt. Baldy's notorious flatwall section, April 1989; Taking it to the Badlands, Dave Duncan hucks a burly mute air at the Pipeline, September 1988; Time to grind.*

Clockwise from top left: *Steve Douglas pushes through a proper Smith grind at Raging Waters, September 1987; Oahu's famed Wallos Spillway has hosted many skate gatherings over the years. Hawaiian renegade Billy Deans attacks one of its cascading hips with a speedy melon lien grab, June 1987; Guerrero (con sombrero) strikes an acoustic number, November 1988.*

Street Style, Red Dog, Damage & Chaos

By Fausto Vitello

Skateboarding was booming in the mid- to late '80s. The ramp scene had exploded, and everybody was skatin'. For KT and me, the scene had gotten kind of stale, though; every ramp was pretty much the same, and, more important, a vibrant street scene was developing in our neck of the woods.

In SF, 9th Avenue was the center of the skate universe. Tommy Guerrero and his boys ruled that turf. It was obvious to me that if skateboarding was going to take the next leap, street skating had to be pushed to the forefront.

I did the first street style contest at Golden Gate Park. It was behind the old Conservatory of Flowers that modern-day street style got its start. KT and I built some crude jump ramps, and that was it. As soon as people showed up, we knew it was a hit. Everybody was hyped, and the skating was like nothing seen before.

I don't quite remember how it happened, but soon after the contest, I hooked up with James Muir, AKA "Red Dog." He was running Dogtown Skates and had a band of notorious skaters, led by Eric Dressen. Red Dog and I became close friends and then business partners.

Red Dog was having problems in Venice, so he decided to move to SF. With him on board, building all kinds of ramps became easy. He is a magician with a Skil saw and a hammer. We hooked up with shops or whoever would have us and threw street contests. The ramps we built at Savannah, Capitola, Sacramento, and other places are still pretty much what people use today. The central ramp at Savannah, which was mostly the work of Red Dog, KT, and Lance Mountain, became kind of the centerpiece of street contests.

The contests were great, but what really shook up the world was the partying that went on during them, particularly at Savannah. It was total chaos; people could barely make it to the events. There was no end to the damage we did: we destroyed countless hotels; Miles Orkin, then an editor at *Thrasher*, set himself on fire while downing shots of 151 rum; Red Dog and others trapped me, naked and with only a blunt to occupy me, on a hotel balcony; and Bob Denike went to jail for defending skaters' rights.

What made all this happen was Independent and *Thrasher*. Most of the industry thought that nothing could replace vert. Well, as always, the skaters have the final say. As the '80s became the '90s, many major manufacturers saw their demise. From those ashes rose the current wave of skateboarding, led by the notorious Steve Rocco … but that's another story.

Above: *Dave Hackett, definitive snap-back gnarler at Gonzo's, May 1988. Below: Going for make or break, Danny Sargent crails a wheeler in a pocket of functional 'crete, November 1988.*

Above: *Including the centerpiece, Savannah Slamma's street course laid the foundation for things to come. Right: Jim Muir and Christian Hosoi, August 1987.*

WANTED

CRAIG JOHNSON

✠ Bounty paid by Independent Truck Co. ✠

Texas hot shoe Craig Johnson was a wanted man who stayed true to the real deal, August 1990.

Above: *Venerable disciple and advocate of Indy's big 215s, Brian Brannon rasps a lot of axle across a square-lipped backyard pit in Tempe, AZ, January 1987.*
Below: *A rare and custom sweatshirt with a chromed FW design; A stage VI tee.*

Clockwise from top left: *Ricky Barnes uncovers his permanent Indy wristwatch, April 1990; It's never too late for Salba Claus. Holiday*

Little Frankie Hill goes big with an ollie to fakie outside the Powell-Peralta compound, November 1989.

Above: *With his tranny skills on point, Jason Lee seizes a tail grab on a pair of sapphire Stage Vs, October 1990.*

Below, from left: *Taking the streets to the next level, Henry Sanchez blasts a nose grind across the Sears curb, October 1990; On any Sunday afternoon, you could find Ray Meyer doing his thing in San Francisco's Golden Gate Park; December 1989; Jeff "Ffej" Hedges extends his handplant reputation with a full-tilt Andrecht in Los Angeles, 1990.*

1/87 *Steve Caballero*

2/87 *Lance Mountain*

3/87 *Bryce Kanights*

4/87 *Brian Brannon*

5/87 *Rob Roskopp*

6/87

7/87 *Don Brown*

8/87 *Christian Hosoi*

9/87

10/87

11/87 *Hosoi & Caballero*

12/87 *Jeff Grosso*

1/88 *Tommy Guerrero*

2/88

3/88 *Eric Dressen*

4/88 *Rob Roskopp*

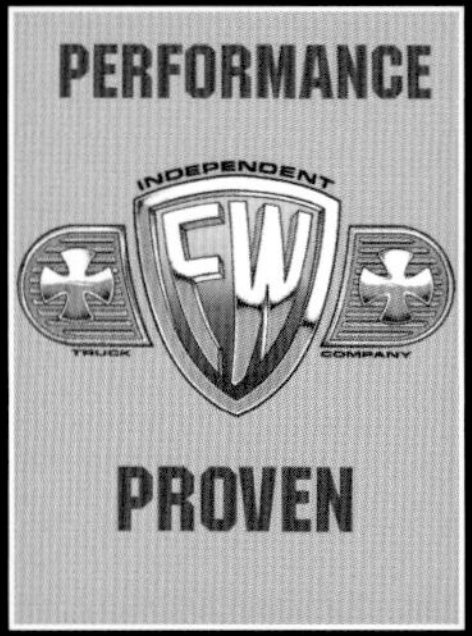

5/88

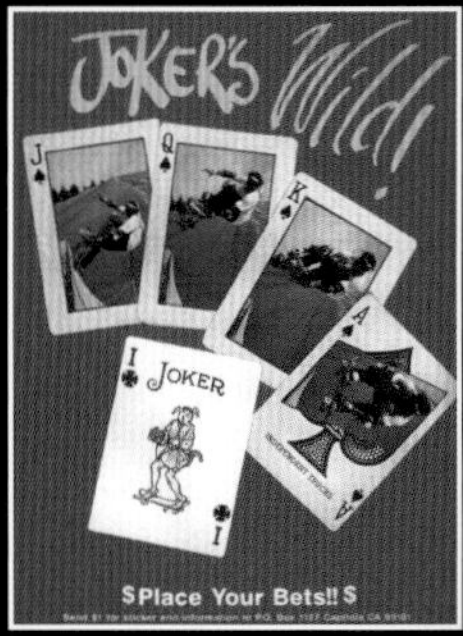

6/88 *Steve Steadham*

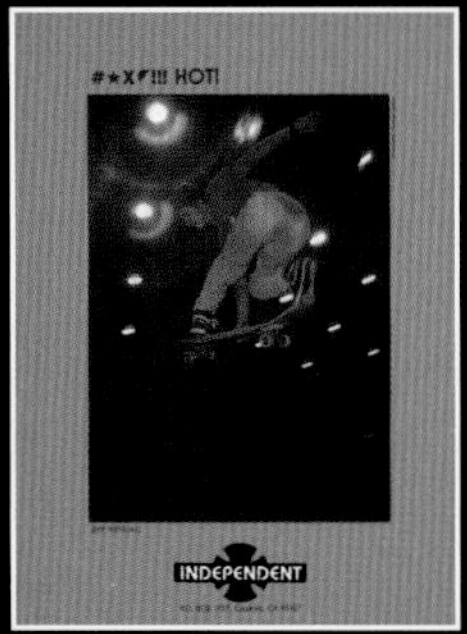

7/88 *Jeff Kendall*

8/88 *Andy Howell*

9/88 *Scott Oster*

10/88 *Jim Murphy*

11/88

12/88 *Christian Hosoi*

1/89 *Doug Smith*

2/89 *Rodney Mullen*

3/89 *Eric Dressen*

4/89

5/89 *Tommy Guerrero*

6/89 *Lori Rigsby*

7/89 *Steve Caballero*

8/89 *Jeff Kendall*

8/89 *Lance Mountain*

9/89 *Tom Knox*

11/89 *Christian Hosoi*

12/89 *Eric Dressen*

1/90 *Danny Sargent*

2/90 *Jim Murphy*

3/90 *Micke Alba*

4/90 *Tommy Guerrero*

5/90 *Mark Gonzales*

6/90

7/90

8/90 *Craig Johnson*

9/90 *Steve Alba*

10/90 *Tom Knox*

11/90 *John Lucero*

12/90 *Scott Oster*

ad archive
1987-1990

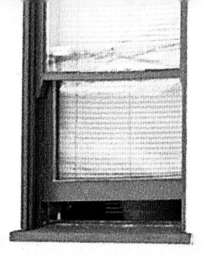

Hesh vs. Fresh,
Slash Dog vs. Tech ✠✠✠✠

By Joey Tershay

As the '90s progressed, skateboarding regressed. Equipment changed monthly, and wheels, which had been 66 mm at their largest in the '80s, got as small as 38 mm. Boards that had been nine or ten inches wide and shaped like fish, with giant tails and short noses, became eight-inch-wide pill-shaped decks with noses longer than the tail. To compensate, trucks also started getting narrow.

Since there were no cement parks left and wooden ramps were only found in a few people's backyards, street skating was the only form of skateboarding that was accessible on a daily basis. Old freestylers started taking over the industry

1991-1996

In a spontaneously raw display, Coco Santiago blasts across a steep driveway gap and gets away with it, October 1993.

"I don't see how you quit skateboarding. You just don't quit skateboarding until you can't physically do it anymore."

—Tommy Guerrero

A launch ramp is just a launch ramp, and really what matters is how you use it. Tommy Guerrero draws a high line above a schoolyard bench with assistance, October 1995.

by creating fresh new brands and distribution companies. Vertical skating and its disciples were laid to rest, while street skating created its own new culture by combining the technical aspects of freestyle with the aggression of vert and bowl riding. As this new wave began to dominate in the mid-'90s, new and riskier tricks developed on a daily basis, replacing street skating moves that had occurred mostly on curbs and ledges and imitated established vertical maneuvers. Skaters started substituting kickflips for basic street ollies and doing flip tricks over anything they had simply ollied in the past. Switch-stance skating also developed during that era, marking the beginning of the end for one-directional skateboarding.

The industry pushed aside old vert pros to make room for a new generation of kids advancing the sport on an urban level. As city streets became the new skateparks, this evolution quickly fueled a rivalry between vert and street skaters. Seventies skaters were mostly clean-cut surfer types; the '80s hit with punk rock; and the '90s ushered in the era of hip-hop, rave, and baggy jeans. Hesh vs. fresh, slashdog vs. tech. Size-XXL T-shirts and size-40-waist pants became the fashion. High-top shoes were cut into low tops, and style flew out the window.

Videos also entered the picture, and soon magazines were using video-grabbed sequences instead of print film. Consistency began to supercede ability, and making the trick was all that seemed to matter—whether you rolled away smoothly or even landed it clean. Only a few contests took place, and none of them offered major prize money. A lot of old pros were forced to find regular jobs.

Although by the mid-'90s, street skating had established itself as the basis of skateboarding, vert started to crawl out of its hole as televised contests emerged and new technical flip tricks and switch skating flowed into the vert domain. Finally, skateboarding had an opportunity for unity and boundless limits.

Companies were still small, however, and skaters piled into vans with their own money and hit the road, supporting themselves by selling product out of their trunks. Road trips, as the sole means of touring, helped rebuild the underground skate community, a strong culture that continues to rebel against the laws of normal day-to-day life. Skating has always been able to adapt to an ever-changing environment and its own unique playground. Skaters can go anywhere on the planet, hook up with another brother on their wooden shred sled, and share a common bond. The language of Skate and Destroy is universal.

Board graphics did not share such commonality. During the mid-'90s, images associated with specific pros changed every couple of months. Favoring graphic and logo parodies, companies bit artwork from sodas, candy, automobiles, supermarkets, religions, and even their own competition. Finally, some companies stopped producing pro models and graphics altogether, and those blank decks put a huge dent in the skateboard economy. Pros were paid base salaries as low as a hundred bucks a month with no royalties.

Searching for industry support, skaters turned increasingly to videos for exposure. Tricks had always been promoted via word of mouth, but magazines couldn't keep up with all the new moves. Videos were more convenient, and "sponsor me" tapes became young hopefuls' preferred method of hooking themselves up. Every suburban kid must have made a tape.

Throughout these transitions, Independent Truck Company has always been the backbone of skateboarding. Indy riders have piloted all world records thrown down on a skateboard and have helped transform the whole of skateboarding culture. Independent's image and riders, and the trucks' three-point fulcrum technology and uncompromising geometry, are the standard the rest of the industry is measured by. They truly are Built to Grind.

Left to right: *Heads or tails, it's still The Gonz. Floaty frontside air at Ray Rodriguez' ramp, October 1990; Even with a torn palm, he's still stoked, February 1999.* Opposite page: *Gonz clears a notorious curb cut with an ollie impossible deep in Santa Monica, 1991.*

mark GONZALES

"Independent trucks are all about turning, and turning is the essence of skateboarding." —Mark Gonzales

Probably nothing and almost definitely nobody better represents what it is to skateboard than Mark Gonzales. Countless people have said it before; countless people will say it again: Gonz and all he has done will forever echo in the halls of skating.

Mark knows, probably better than anybody else does, what it means to skate everything. He can stretch a Madonna, whip a switch 360 flip, or lipslide a rail with equal ease and style, and, more important, he can do 100 things you never even thought of before, and 95 of those tricks are probably completely spontaneous. Whether it was the first purposely executed switch-stance skateboarding, the first double-kink rail, bringing the kick-flip to the streets, or just opening up the way we all see skateboarding in general, The Gonz has been pioneering since the day he stepped on a board. Who knows where we'd all be without him? Mark has made it all more creative, more dangerous, more inspirational, and, most important, more fun. *—Mark Whiteley for* Slap *magazine, December 2003, Issue #139*

I vividly remember the first time I skated with Mark Gonzales; Neil Blender, Ed Templeton, Mike Vallely, Natas Kaupas, and a 15 year-old Chris Pastras were all there. We were skating these little vert banks at a bank in Costa Mesa, CA. I had never skated there before that night, but it was apparently a big spot in Orange County, and Mark and Neil frequented it. Mark didn't just skate really well that night; he was also incredibly encouraging to me. His infectious energy gave me the strength and the drive to push myself.

Mark's support had a lasting effect on me; from that night on, I felt much more confident about my skating. Coupled with the fact that I was actually skating with Neil and Natas, which was like getting to hang out with The Stones for a night and play guitar with Keith Richards, that night got me going in an entirely new direction. It was worth everything to me, and it still is.

Mark truly set the standard; I felt blessed to be on the Indy team because Mark made everything—including riding Indy trucks—seem right and cool. *—Jason Lee*

I RODE AROUND
WITH MY FRIEND
HE HAD A TORKER,
I HAD MY STEP MOM'S
10 SPEED.
LONG BOARDERS
WOULD SHOOT
DOWN THE HILLS IN
GLENDORA. WE
WENT TO THE
DITCH AND AT
FIRST IT WAS TO

BMX AND THIN
WE REALIZED THAT
IT WAS A SKATESPOT,
SO WE GOT BOARDS
AND WENT BACK.
HE RODE AN ERIC
GRISHAM I RODE
WHO KNOWS WHAT.
SOME PUNK ROCKERS
SHOWED UP AND
ONE HAD AN INDIE

SHURT. THAT
STUCK IN MY
HEAD I RIDE
INDEPENDENTS
CAUS WHEN I
AM ONTOP OF
THE BOARD
I LIKE TO STAY
CENTRAL AND
BALANCED...
Mark Gonzales

LIKE THE LOGO IS JUN 11 03

194

This page, clockwise from above: *Mark takes the high road to self-service in San Francisco, September 2000; Crossing the channel at Ripon Skatepark with a super-boosted frontside boneless, December 2001; In a game of highest kick, you'd certainly lose against Gonzo, December 1997; Speeding along the wrong side of the street in SF, November 1999; Just hanging out in the men's room, August 1998.*

Opposite, from far left: *Gonz has always had mad love for the vertical realm, and this five-foot backside ollie at the Fallbrook Ramp proves it, September 1989; Mark's versatile and catlike ability shines through on this light-footed no comply, January 2000.*

colin McKAY ✠✠✠✠

"Indy symbolizes longevity; it's the most hardcore skateboard company in existence today." —Colin McKay

From a very early age, Colin McKay was kicking up a racket with his skateboarding skill and keen awareness. He progressed rapidly at his local skatepark, the Skate Ranch, in Richmond, BC. Before he hit puberty, Colin possessed a grip of transition and ramp skills that few kids his age or older could match. Over the course of three years, Colin's skating was featured in several Powell Peralta videos: *Public Domain, Ban This,* and *Propaganda.*

In 1992, looking for a change of pace and taking advantage of an undeniable opportunity, Colin signed on with the now-legendary Plan B team Although he is widely regarded as one of the most technically skilled and creative vert skaters in the world, he also had a technical flair for urban terrain early on and made waves by applying modern street tricks to the vertical plane. His crossover abilities were especially remarkable in some of the best videos of all time: Plan B's *Questionable, Virtual Reality,* and *Second Hand Smoke.*

Colin is a longtime member of the Independent team, except for a brief period of disillusionment in 1996 when he strayed to endorse another truck brand (although he claims he never actually rode them). This minor infraction aside, Colin has always been proud to be a part of a crew of people who have integrity and skateboarding longevity.

As skateboarding's mainstream popularity soared in the new millennium, Colin's style and appeal earned him a few high-profile television appearances, including a handful of skating clips riding a halfpipe high atop a Manhattan skyscraper and a much-discussed cameo in a commercial with Alyssa Milano.

Colin is a seasoned and proficient master of the rolling wooden plank, and few other vert skaters possess his tenacity and boundless technical abilities. Since the days when accessorizing skateboards with plastic was popular, Colin has been making his indelible mark on skateboarding.

—Bryce Kanights

Clockwise from top: *Colin lays down the licks with a proper switch hardflip, Vancouver, BC, September 1996; Don't scratch the paint, May 1995; Richmond's Skate Ranch directly affected Colin's progress as a little kid, as evidenced by this confident nosebone transfer, August 1988.*

Opposite page, clockwise from top left: *Twisted frontside noseslide atop the Skate Street vert ramp, January 1998; Colin clutches a face-high frontside tail grab at the privately skated, yet publicly renowned, Plan B Ramp, February 1996; At the Mexican border, Colin's highest air measures 13 feet, August 1997; Half Cab heelflip on the banks of Vancouver's rarely dehydrated Georgia street fountain, October 1994.*

WAY ✠✠✠✠

"If you're not in tune with your trucks, everything is out of tune." —Danny Way

What makes Danny Way such a legendary skateboarder? Is it his ability to disregard fear as little more than a nuisance? Or is it some inherent talent that has empowered him to overcome obstacles that would normally be insurmountable in skateboarding?

Danny's unusual approach to skating started at age 11, when he decided to learn difficult tricks like the gay twist and the Madonna on our backyard halfpipe—before he could perform simpler tricks like proper backside airs and regular inverts. By age 12, Danny's unconventional approach propelled him to victory in his first 1A-CASL contest at Del Mar Skate Ranch. Judges and spectators alike were stunned to see this preteen rolling into the keyhole pool and exiting with frontside airs, rock and rolls, and backside bonelesses on coping. There was much more to come.

Danny made his way through the CASL circuit and progressed rapidly through the ranks. He was picked up by Alexander's Skate Shop (which later became Pacific Drive) and, in no time, landed himself a sponsorship with Hosoi Skateboards for his street skating. He adjusted easily to new challenges and competition in street and vert contests. After competing in a series of amateur contests, and after some sponsorship changes over the course of about three years between Vision, Hosoi, and Powell Peralta, he ultimately found himself on H-Street Skateboards. He won at the Houston NSA amateur vert contest when he was 15, and H-Street turned him pro. Competing against the big boys, he placed an admirable second in his first pro street contest and won his first-ever pro vert contest.

Danny got quite a buzz going in the skateboard world by beating out industry greats like Tony Hawk, Christian Hosoi, Jason Lee, and Mark Gonzales—all former team members, idols, and mentors. It was the era of the super team: small, tight-knit crews packed with extraordinary talent and focus. After a quick stint on Blind, Danny joined forces with Michael Ternasky, Rodney Mullen, Mike Carroll, Rick Howard, Pat Duffy, and others, who had just formed the soon-to-be-infamous Plan B program.

Danny thrived in his new environment, and he and the Plan B team dominated the industry media by creating epic videos and setting new benchmarks in skateboarding. By 1993, when Danny was voted *Thrasher* magazine's Skater of the Year, he had definitely secured his status as a skateboarding legend.

Danny continues pioneering various ramp configurations and stunts and posing new challenges for future skateboarders. In 1997, he broke the world record for highest air at 16 feet, six inches. Then he bomb-dropped out of a hovering helicopter into the same monstrous ramp just for fun, scoring the cover and a full feature in *Transworld*. In 2002, he broke another world record with a 65-foot method air that shattered the previous longest air mark. The next day, sore and bruised, he pressed on and broke his own high air record by nailing a 50-foot backside 360 across a straight jump into a lofty 18-foot backside air above the 20-plus-foot quarter pipe.

In 2003, Danny landed a series of tricks rarely or never seen before on a skateboard. Blasting down a huge roll-in and over 50- to 75-foot gaps, Danny stomped frontside 360 heelflips, frontside 540s, switch frontside 540s, switch backside 360s, backside 540 tail grabs, and off-axis backside 720s. He followed up these groundbreaking maneuvers with a record-crushing 23-and-a-half-foot backside air and a slew of technical flip and

Stare at this photo for a minute and put yourself in Danny's shoes. Kind of sickening, isn't it? Danny shatters all previous high air records with this 23.5-foot backside blaster. The ramp's transition is 25 feet with two feet of vertical. How high is he above the desert floor? You do the math, June 12, 2003.

varial tricks out of the 27-foot-high quarter pipe. To Danny, this series of unimaginable feats merely represented a checklist of personal goals.

Throughout his career, Danny has pushed limits, won numerous contests, set records, and redefined skateboarding's possibilities. He has paid for his successes with a slew of injuries that would have ended less tenacious skaters' careers. But Danny's impenetrable conviction and relentless perseverance have always set him apart. And as long as he can continue building his legacy, he will inevitably continue guiding skateboarding to new frontiers. —Damon Way

Clockwise from top left: Danny scorches a 12-foot method above the twilight glow of the DC mega-ramp, August 2001; With what are certainly the best Madonnas in the business, DW prepares for the smackdown at the Encinitas Y, September 1999; Blasted method transfer from bowl to snake run at Kona Skatepark, Jacksonville, FL, September 1991; Adaptive towards any environment, Danny gaps out to crooks in San Diego County, December 2002.

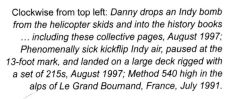

Clockwise from top left: *Danny drops an Indy bomb from the helicopter skids and into the history books ... including these collective pages, August 1997; Phenomenally sick kickflip Indy air, paused at the 13-foot mark, and landed on a large deck rigged with a set of 215s, August 1997; Method 540 high in the alps of Le Grand Bournand, France, July 1991.*

"We didn't like Danny Way much when he was a little kid; we were extremely jealous of his talent, I'd have to say. As we watched Danny coming up, we thought, 'This is the kid who's going to knock us all over.'" —Jeff Grosso

tim
BRAUCH ✠✠✠✠

Have you ever had a friend who just has natural flair? It's not something you can buy at the store to be hip; it's real. This person never complains; he is motivated and down to party, and he'll hype up the session so much that his energy becomes contagious. And when he skates, he skates everything in his path, be it a rail, stairs, a pool, or a vert ramp. Enter Tim Brauch.

Tim fucking rips. We call him "Beans," because when he skates, he bounces off the walls like a jumping bean. Pop! Pop! Pop! Although Tim is glued to his skateboard, his attack is sporadic; even he never seems to know what he'll do next. He can turn a bail into a trick and keep going. And his tricks are some of the craziest I've seen; he can 50–50 a rail to varial mute out.

Tim is best known for being able to do any blunt trick known to man: blunt kickflip to Indy nosepick; blunt to tail in some crazy pools; 5-0 to blunt on a handrail. I would not bullshit you. He's the reason why I do blunts.

Skating aside, Tim is also an all-around nice guy. One of San Jose's finest, he holds highest honors in the B.M.C. And now you know what natural flair means. It means Tim Brauch. Homies for life! T.B.M.C. —*Crooks (Chet Childress)*

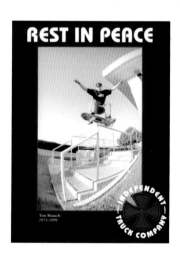

REST IN PEACE

Tim Brauch
1974-1999

INDEPENDENT TRUCK COMPANY

"Tim is my 'roll' model. Whenever I reach one of life's little impasses, I ask myself, 'What would Tim do?'" —Ron Whaley

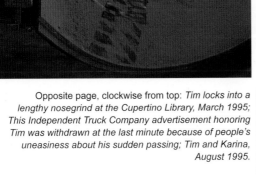

Opposite page, clockwise from top: *Tim locks into a lengthy nosegrind at the Cupertino Library, March 1995; This Independent Truck Company advertisement honoring Tim was withdrawn at the last minute because of people's uneasiness about his sudden passing; Tim and Karina, August 1995.*

Clockwise from top left: *Suited as Forrest Gump, Tim's resemblance to Tom Hanks was a sure shot for this moment, December 1996; Loading dock melon launch, April 1997; Another fine catch by Beans, September 1998; On road trips, Tim and his crew often morphed motel rooms into playgrounds, June 1996; Roommates then and friends forever, Tim and Jason Adams kick it at home, May 1993; With every variation of the trick in his possession, Tim was known as the most blunted skateboarder ever. Tim works his magic at the Third Street Ramp in downtown San Jose, October 1998.*

STAGE VII

Original Release Date: February 1993
Available Sizes: 136, 146, 156, 166
Other Trucks Available: Stage I 101, Stage IV 215
Available Colors: Silver
Features: Added 136 Size, Reduced Material on Hanger, Beefed-Up Pivot Housing, Added Modern Mounting Hole Pattern

STAGE VII
136 mm

• Original logo concepts like this Built to Grind cross artwork would be mocked up and hand-colored to decide color-ways for stickers and tees.

• Rick Blackhart conceived a character named "Truckie" that was partially developed but never utilized.

• This eagle graphic, which originally appeared on a team shirt for the Back to the City street contest in San Francisco, 1993, was faxed to NHS to be cleaned up for a sticker.

• This pant illustration shows a patch application on a pair of denim jeans.

artifacts
1991-1996

- Over the years, many bootleg tees have turned up. This "Indica" bootleg is a team favorite.

- This idea for a Stage VII logo would have represented a digression from usual Roman numeral numbering, and it was never utilized.

- These three comp sketches of cartoonish logos were considered too corny for Independent and were never developed.

- An original layout for an Independent beanie was first drawn up and then patterned by the beanie manufacturer.

- This "Viva Independiente" tee was developed for a big skate contest in Mexico that never happened— Long Live Independent!

- Some classic OGBC logo patches.

BIG BAR STICKER
7" WIDE (2 COLOR COMBOS)
MED BAR 4" WIDE (2 COLOR COMBOS)

NEW BAR & CROSS

SHIRT
PUT BLACK BORDER
AROUND BAR & CROSS.

- Joey Tershay would submit requests to NHS for stickers and tees. This one calls out sticker sizes and shows a logo application for a tee, with options for color backgrounds.

- This style sheet shows the initial process of applying sticker or T-shirt art to a cap.

Brian Ferdinand
skids through a
rapid noseblunt slide
at UC Berkeley's
Sproul Plaza,
March 1992.

Above: *In Orlando, FL, Julien Stranger clears a wide void between the bricks while the security guards hit up the donut shop, May 1992.*
Right: *Produced in limited quantities, a match-up of select brass pins.*

photo archive
1991-1996

BRIAN LOTTI

Brian Lotti kicks into this Independent ad with a lofty one-footed ollie. Thrasher, June 1992.

Clockwise from top left: *Salman Agah flicks one to fakie at Bruno's bank, February 1994; Kevin Rucks tosses a late egg at the afternoon sky in Corvallis, OR, July 1991; Rick Ibaseta gives a useless pedestrian guard rail a purpose, November 1992; Mark "Red" Scott commits to a boneless reentry in Corvallis, OR, July 1991.*

Opposite page: *Young Lavar McBride came up big at many of San Francisco's street spots. This photo of him was slated to be on the cover of* Thrasher *until the little man sprayed about it to all his homies. It's usually best to be patient until the cake is fully baked, September 1993.*

Clockwise from above left: *If only it were an operational cop car; Mike Daher snaps into a fender bender in Venice Beach, CA, August 1994; The raging firestorm that hit the Oakland and Berkeley hills in 1991 left well over 30 backyard gems in its aftermath. Southland visitor Remy Stratton stretches a lofty ollie "seatbelt" grab at the heavily skated Black Bottom Pool, August 1992; Noah Salasnek finds the time and space to get in your face at Studio 43, June 1991.*

"If you don't care about money anymore, if you don't care about endorsements, if you don't care about getting an ad, I think you ride Indys. It's the truth." —Mark Gonzales

Above: *Always up for a challenge, John Cardiel goes the distance on a mammoth ramp transfer in Brussels, Belgium, August 1996.*
Left: *The Independent "check" T-shirt.*

Mike Schwartz took command of lengthy rails long before it became routine. Thrasher, *December 1992.*

Denice Vaughn Kilik,
Built to Grind,
September 1994.

Above: Frozen in a paradigmatic tre flip, Kien Lieu activates a late-afternoon shadowbox, November 1994. Right: A saintly team tee.

Top: *Evading security forces, Brad Staba reaps the rewards of a kickflip on the rise of a highway construction project, August 1996.* Bottom, from left: *A very imaginative Simon Woodstock becomes the obvious target at Derby Park, October 1993; Pulling out a classic cue from his immense collection, Chicken gives it some love in his backyard, October 1991; Salba stalls an Anchrecht for good measure at Bellmar's pool, February 1995.*

"Catching a glimpse of Julien is like seeing Bigfoot. He is so under the radar. He'll go skate by himself, and you'll hear about sightings: 'I heard Julien did this or that.' He is so damn good." —Tommy Guerrero

Old stomping grounds become new meat for Julien Stranger on a frontside noseblunt slide, Benicia, CA, 1996.

Above: *Barker Barrett locks in and laps over the death chamber at Chicken's pool, September 1995;* Right: *Another backside Smith grind, this time on a tall flat bar by Portland's Matt Beach, July 1996.*

Clockwise from left: *Chad Muska manifests the hurricane madness, August 1995; Burning bright since 1978; When dealt the hot hand, Darren Navarrette keeps it burning true and through, June 1996.*

The ever-controversial and spooky "Possessed" ad. Slap, January 1995.

"Skateboarding led me to a point where I became totally free. The whole DIY attitude of skateboarding pretty much made me who I am today." —Tommy Guerrero

Above: *King of the hills, Tommy Guerrero takes the express route down a San Francisco sidewalk, October 1995.*
Right: *Bowl builder and destroyer Mark "Monk" Hubbard powers across a doorway channel in Sattel, Switzerland, July 1995.*

Above: *The Sanctuary Pool hosted numerous skate sessions off and on in its day, and pool missionary Royce Nelson traveled the long road just to attack this gem's flawless transitions. Tuck knee outshines stinkbug every time, August 1996.* Left: *Pete Colpitts' rendered silver dollar cross necklace, crafted by the dedicated hands of his friend Alan Bisgaard.*

Clockwise from top left: *Fausto hits SF's Pac Bell banks, 1980; At the Pipeline, Jerry Hurtado zips through the banked reservoir, 1988; John Dettman-Lytle unscrambles an egg at the Kennedy warehouse, 1990; A worldly Joey Tershay clocks in for duty under an overpass near Mexico City, 2002; Doctor Rick Blackhart unleashes into a frontside lipslide at Greer Park, 1992.*

Not the Average Daily Grind

The Team Managers

Being the team manager for Independent Trucks isn't a normal position that you interview for; one day you just realize you have the job. There are no prerequisites, other than Indy pride and the ability to roll. Using Jay Shuirman's initial philosophy of "letting skaters be skaters," Fausto Vitello built the infrastructure of the team and mobilized the majority of early big-name riders. After running a company and growing *Thrasher* magazine became too much for Fausto to handle on his own, he recruited Jerry "Taters" Hurtado to assist him in the early '80s. Taters took care of guys like Duane, who sometimes needed a little extra help getting from wherever he was sleeping to the contest in time for his first run. A half-dozen years later, skater and magazine production staffer John Dettman stepped into the role to assist with team packages and ad layouts. Ultimately, Fausto's former professional badass and original Indy test pilot, Rick Blackhart, became the first full-time team manager and spent the greater part of the late '80s slinging product and assembling a diverse crew of heavy-hitting Independent devotees. And beginning in the early '90s, Joey Tershay rolled up to the hefty position, in which he's now worked alongside hundreds of skateboarders for over a decade. —*K.W.*

"Riding for Indy was great ... working for Indy sucked, period." —**Rick Blackhart**

"You could say I was in the right place at the right time or the wrong place at the right time." —**Joey Tershay**

"Christian Hosoi always skates fast and high. I've watched him do stuff that no one could ever do, and he's not even conscious of it. It's just a natural gift."

—Tommy Guerrero

Above: *Cruising in burgundy brotherhood, Darren Navarrette keeps his eyes on the prize while Al Partanen and Sam Hitz ponder a destination unknown, April 1996.*
Left: *Christian Hosoi blasts a monumental benihana at Bellmar's pool, September 1996.*

mountain

Lance Mountain's last ad as an Independent team rider was perhaps his best. Late egg at the Girl ramp, shot by Rick Howard. Thrasher, June 1996.

Thrasher magazine ▶

1/91

2/91 *Jason Lee*

3/91 *Mike Youssefpour*

4/91 *Mike Crescini*

5/91 *Sal Barbier*

6/91 *Jason Rogers*

7/91 *Ray Barbee*

8/91 *Mike Carroll*

9/91 *Tommy Guerrero*

10/91 *James Kelch*

11/91

12/91 *Steve Caballero*

1/92 *Christian Hosoi*

2/92 *Salman Agah*

3/92 *Brian Ferdinand*

4/92 *Rick Ibaseta*

5/92 *Danny Way*

6/92 *Brian Lotti*

7/92 *Chet Thomas*

8/92 *Kris Markovich*

9/92 *Gershon Mosley*

10/92 *Chris Senn*

11/92 *Frank Hirata*

12/92 *Mike Schwartz*

1/93 *Salman Agah*

2/93

3/93 *Jordan Richter*

4/93 *Simon Woodstock*

5/93 *Danny Sargent*

6/93 *Rick Howard*

7/93 *Rob Boyce*

8/93 *Ocean Howell*

9/93 *Omar Hassan*

10/93 *Colin McKay*

11/93 *Tommy Guerrero*

12/93 *Kris Markovich*

1/94 *Carl Shipman*

2/94 *Duane Peters*

3/94 *Mike Daher*

4/94 *Gabriel Rodriguez*

5/94 *Coco Santiago*

6/94 *Julien Stranger*

7/94 *Remy Stratton*

8/94 *Kien Lieu*

9/94 *Rick Ibaseta*

10/94 *Tim Brauch*

11/94 *Mike Crum*

12/94 *Christian Hosoi*

1/95 *Ricky Oyola*

2/95 *Rick Howard*

3/95 *Sal Barbier*

4/95 *Jeff Taylor*

5/95 *Salman Agah*

6/95 *Mike Frazier*

7/95 *Tas & Ben Pappas*

8/95 *Ray Barbee*

9/95 *Danny Way*

10/95 *Tim Brauch*

11/95 *Rene Mattheysen*

12/95 *Moses Itkonen*

1991-1996 ad archive

Thrasher magazine ▶

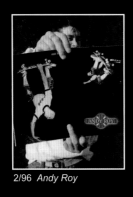

1/96 *Chad Muska*

2/96 *Andy Roy*

3/96 *Ethan Fowler*

4/96 *Peter Hewitt*

5/96 *Skip Pronier*

6/96 *Lance Mountain*

7/96 *Coco Santiago*

8/96 *Rudy Johnson*

9/96 *Sean Young*

10/96

11/96 *Chet Thomas*

12/96 *Bob Burnquist*

Slap ▶

4/92 *Chad Jackson*

5/92
Mike Cao

6/92

7/92

8/92 *Adam McNatt*

9/92
Quy Nguyen

10/92

12/92

1/93 *Edward Devera*

4/93 *Mike Frazier*

2/93
Royce Nelson

3/93
Mike York

5/93
Mike Schwartz

6/93
Jeff Taylor

7/93 *Papo*

8/93
Brian Chung

8/93
Joe Sierro

10/93

11/93
Jeff Reeves

12/93

1/94
Sean Young

2/94

3/94
Chico Brenes

4/94
Max Schaaf

Slap ▶

7/94 *Drake Jones*

8/94 *Jason Adams*

9/94 *Jamie Thomas*

10/94 *Weston Correa*

11/94 *Chad Fernandez*

12/94 *Sean Young*

1/95

2/95 *Jesse Driggs*

3/95 *Eric Jay*

4/95 *Mike Judd*

5/95 *Ben Sanchez*

7/95 *Brian Chung*

7/95 *Aaron Astorga*

8/95

9/95 *Mike Daher*

10/95 *Greg Hunt*

11/95 *Joe Sierro*

12/95 *Justin Pierce*

1/96 *Barker Barrett*

2/96 *Darren Navarrette*

3/96 *Osage Buffalo*

4/96 *Gabriel Rodriguez*

5/96 *Justin Strubing*

6/96 *Chad Fernandez*

7/96 *Brian Duke*

8/96 *Drake Jones*

9/96 *Peter Hewitt*

10/96 *Moses Itkonen*

11/96

12/96 *Matt Beach*

1991-1996 ad archive

There Will Always Be Diehards

✠ ✠ ✠ ✠

By Lance Dawes

And so went the going as the new millennium crept into sight. Even though the future looked brighter than 80,000 lighters at Ozzfest, coming events would begin to twist the skate world into knots. The term "too big for your britches" comes to mind. The physical act of skating continually moved forward, but skating became bigger than just feeling the wind in one's hair—big money started to take over and create unwanted influence. Regardless, the skaters managed to stay true and pushed and shoved their abilities to all-time highs.

Big stunts became the rage and pulled the rest of the world up front and center. Bigger was better, and a few psychos laid it down for the rest to ponder with dropped jaws. Danny Way, the lone wolf of pure power vert skating, shocked the world by blasting over 17 feet above the coping to set a new world record. On a set of Indy 215s, he also jumped into the same ramp via Indy air from the precarious skids of a hovering helicopter. Tony Hawk landed the elusive 900 in 1999 and began whipping them out on an ongoing basis. A Brazilian force by the name of Bob Burnquist took the loop switch in Tampa. Back home, he chopped a section out from the top of his loop structure and switch aired across it. If that wasn't enough, Danny then smashed his previous records by hucking a 75-foot-long 360 air, landing and rolling into history with a 23-and-a-half-foot backside air.

With all this testosterone of youth culture flying around, the world stood on its toes and took notice—especially corporate America. From '97 to 2003 and beyond, skateboarding has seen more outsiders stopping by to cash in than ever before—with and without the help of skaters. Some got rich, some got fat, some got jacked, and others just burned out. But the streets are where the tough and true skaters remain to thrive. The mainstream media has only scratched the surface, for all the real skaters are still living outside the law, sticking to the search and destroy mantra. And with skateboarding's flourishing popularity has emerged the once-revered concrete skatepark. These facilities are a good idea in theory, but today's skateparks have become the community's excuse to herd us into one place, control us, and fill their quota books. Variety at a price.

In the realm of skatepark design and construction, the truly dedicated skaters are leading the pack and paving the way. Physical examples of what should and can be done have been designed and built by the impervious minds and hands of the Dreamland and Grindline crews in the Northwest. These functional forms attest to their core competency and brilliance.

At the street level, skaters continue to prod the system. More like urban guerrillas, these skaters take their cue from the

Skaters used to look at this rail (now capped) and wonder how it could be skated. Dustin Dollin resolved the issue with a sharp carve from a short run up. No other truck can do that for you, Melbourne, Australia, November 2001.

1997-2003

Howard Cooke and James Woodsley
double up with amusement in a yard of
discarded cylinders in Portland, OR.
October 2001.

pool pirates before them and use all means necessary to find skateable terrain. Bolt cutters (or universal keys, as we call them), buckets of Bondo, and Sawzalls are all part of the process, while generators and lights have become the impetus for skating at will. Skateboard photographers and videographers alike have helped to usher in the age of skating anytime, anywhere, and at any expense. Massive rails, tech tricks gone big, and putting one's balls on the line have become the norm, and anything you've seen at the TV Games pales in comparison.

Style and fashion in one form or another have played their parts, and the baggy-panted conformist robots of the early '90s have given way to the motley crews of today. Jim Greco has become a throwback to Duane Peters meets John Grigley, while Tony Trujillo has evoked the spirit of Hosoi and Tony Alva and makes carving look cool and fun again. DIY is back in

vogue, and more mini-ramps, backyard bowls and vert ramp monstrosities are popping up daily. Getting rich hasn't corrupted everyone. The purists remain stoked and fueled by their bros, coveted skate spots, buds, and suds.

As the future rushes toward us, faster every day, skaters will surely survive, adapt, and prosper. No matter how we progress—whether monetarily, mentally, or by sheer volume—a skater is a skater for life. Our world has changed tenfold since skateboarding began, but few things have remained constant. There will always be diehards, the ones always looking ahead, searching for the unimaginable and the unclaimed. Whether in backyard pools or skateparks, or on sidewalks, hills, banks, or hubba ledges, there will always be 'crete. And no matter what, there will always be one skateboard truck worth riding that has the history and attitude to get you there—so ride the best, fuck the rest. Viva Independent!

REYNOLDS ✠ ✠ ✠ ✠

From left: *The boss takes his 15-minute break; Switched-up frontside noseslide on familiar territory in Lakeland, FL, September 2001; Shaggy likeness, July 2001.*

From left: The boss takes his 15-minute break; Switched-up frontside noseslide on familiar territory in Lakeland, FL, September 2001; Shaggy likeness, July 2001.

"Once I rode them, there was no turning back." —Andrew Reynolds

The first thing that struck me about Andrew Reynolds was his incredible ease on a skateboard. He seemed to have been born on it. In the five years that I've been lucky enough to work with Andrew and get to know him as a good friend, I'm still amazed by his ability and natural grace. Andrew rarely leaves the house with a trick in mind and comes home empty handed; riding away from any particular trick he has already committed himself to making is almost like an afterthought. Andrew is a gifted skateboarder in the way that Charlie Parker was a gifted saxophonist or Jimi Hendrix was a gifted guitar player. It's in his blood.

Photographers recognized Andrew's gift early, and as a result, he has been in the public eye for years, steadily pushing the limits of what can be done on four wheels, seven plys of hard rock maple, and a pair of Indys. Thanks to a string of landmark video parts, a few contest victories and awards, and even his own character in former mentor Tony Hawk's video games, Andrew's is one of the most well-known and well-respected names in skateboarding today.

Andrew has achieved this status on his own terms, never seeking out corporate sponsors or resorting to the skateboarder-turned-actor/MTV celebrity route, and he has always forged his popularity on the strength of his skateboarding alone. In 2000, as skateboarding was riding one of its biggest-ever crests in popularity, Andrew started Baker Skateboards. In response to an industry that was clamoring for money and mainstream acceptance, Baker was Andrew's successful attempt to reinject freedom of spirit and rebellious attitude into skateboarding. For Andrew, Independent is more than just a brand of truck he rides or a logo he has tattooed on his arm. It is a description of his philosophy as a skateboarder, a business owner, and a human being. —*Justin Regan*

In the beginning, the kid across the street had a skate magazine. Andrew was seven years old, and he and this kid would spend what seemed like hours looking through this magazine. The next thing we knew, he wanted a skateboard for his birthday. I remember it was a white Mike McGill board with a skeleton and a snake on it. At first I wasn't sure about the picture, and then I realized I didn't care that much. Little did I know at the time that graphics are a big deal in the business.

Andrew would roll around on the board, sitting at first, then standing, and then doing tricks. He really got the hang of it pretty quick. Soon after, a family from Australia with two sons who also skated moved into the neighborhood, and Andrew started skating with them every day after school and on weekends. They would build ramps in the woods, and obstacles started showing up in the driveway. Andrew's stepdad, Ritchie, got involved in building some stuff, and Andrew ended up having everything there was to skate at the house: a rail, launch ramps, a box, and a mini-ramp. Our house became a skatepark of sorts, and the word got around about it. Andrew started hanging out with some older kids who skated, and slowly, a tight-knit skate crew formed around our town.

Andrew was still too young to be going off with older kids, though, so he mainly stuck around the neighborhood. Ritchie used to whistle to get him to come home for supper; one time when he heard the whistle, Andrew came flying down the hill to our house, hit a rock, and ate the pavement really hard. I had to take him to the emergency clinic to have pavement dug out of his face! He was only nine years old at the time.

A big turning point early in Andrew's skateboarding happened when he was 10. We heard about a big contest called the St. Pete Showdown, where all the famous skaters were going to be, and Andrew had to go.

Frozen and infallible in his technique, Andrew catches and readies to set down a massive frontside flip above San Francisco's Big 16, September 2002.

The whole family went, and it was some of the best skating we had ever seen. We were amazed. At that same contest, a booth was set up for the Florida Amateur Skateboard League (FASL). We thought it was great to have something organized for skaters with a contest once a month, each in a different place. We signed Andrew up and saw immediately what incredible talent he had. He went on to win just about every contest FASL had. He was bit intimidated at first, because he was only 10 or 11, and the judges kept bumping him up to the next level, but he was killing it, beating out 17- and 18-year-olds. He loved the success but still managed to stay very humble, even at that early age. Those contests were a good beginning for Andrew's career and for some other great skaters, including Caine Gayle, Jamie Thomas, and Dave Durren.

We couldn't have asked for a better start for Andrew, and as he grew older, we knew he was going in a great direction, so we supported him 100 percent. As a parent, you want your kids to be successful, and I was afraid that Andrew's skateboarding career was going to be short lived. I used to make him apply for jobs at local stores, and we stayed on him about his grades. It was a battle sometimes, because he never liked school, and if he made bad grades, we would take his skateboard away. He would always come around and do better in school because he just couldn't stand it when he couldn't skate. He's still that way today. He eventually graduated from school and left for California at age 17. He had turned pro the previous year, so it only made sense for him to go where the action was.

I guess the rest is history. Skateboarding has given Andrew many opportunities that he would never have had otherwise, including travel, fame, money and some great friends. Andrew has truly been blessed with a great talent. —*Mary Carver* (Andrew's mom)

Clockwise from sequence above: *Simple in its complexity, a back-side kickflip gets handled in LA County, November 2000; This front bluntslide on a renowned rail in Miami helped garner the boss Thrasher's much-coveted S.O.T.Y. status, December 1998; Switch flip in suburbia, September 2002; Andrew springs a 360 flip across the flatlands of Florida, October 2002.*

Opposite: *Another frontside flick, this one snapped high above the gates in Pomona, CA, October 2001.*

Annaka's aging bowl may have been originally built for Japanese '80s gnar dogs, but Peter is one of a very select few able to pilot the airspace high above its deep channel, August 2001.

peter HEWITT ✠ ✠ ✠ ✠

From left: *Locked into a spit-guttered Smith grind at the long-dormant El Cortez Hotel pool, June 1994; Tight tranny? No problem, September 2002; An eggplant gets tossed while the Riverside County Sheriff's boys sniff around the neighborhood for the bona fide criminals, June 2002.*

From left: *Locked into a spit-guttered Smith grind at the long-dormant El Cortez Hotel pool, June 1994; Tight tranny? No problem, September 2002; An eggplant gets tossed while the Riverside County Sheriff's boys sniff around the neighborhood for the bona fide criminals, June 2002.*

"Going faster will make it easier." —Roger Hewitt, Peter's father

In this era of stunt skateboarding, many professionals separate work from fun. They call up their cameramen and make plans to do their big trick once and only once. Then they can relax until the need to bust out strikes again. But Peter Hewitt's approach to skateboarding is different. For him, skateboarding is all fun. He never stresses about tricks or deadlines, and he never makes plans for the "big stunt." Peter just skates full tilt all the time. Most tricks you have seen him do in videos or magazines are ones that he also did before the cameras arrived and that he will do countless times in the future.

Since Peter and his older brother, Paul, first built a quarter pipe in their driveway, skating fast and having fun have been his main priorities. It was his father who told him that "going faster will make it easier," and Peter must have taken those words to heart, because he's one of the fastest in skateboarding. No one gets as high in fullpipes or does frontside 5-0s as far as Hewitt. Many a session has ended with his flying off the end of the ramp. Lately, you can find him skating pools and parks, where there is often no end to the coping.

Whether it's a cross-country road trip with the Hesh Crew in a packed car or a bullet train across Japan, Peter is down to travel. Five-star hotels are nice, but sometimes camping in the sand is more his style. Shying away from contests, Peter would rather session with the locals and impress real skaters than appear on TV and impress the couch potatoes. In person, he always hypes up a session any way he can, whether it's by getting everyone to learn lipslides through the corner or doing the rocket drop-in. His finest moment of the year, however, is Halloween at Burnside. Wearing spandex, pushing mongo, and talking like *Fast Times at Ridgemont High*'s Jeff Spicoli, he has caused many people to wonder if he can snap out of it when the party ends.

One thing Peter hasn't done in skateboarding is make compromises. Avoiding sunglasses, toy, or food sponsors, Peter only chooses product endorsements that are essential to his skating. His all-or-nothing riding style is similarly bare bones. He never does tricks just to get them over with; he does them because he wants to, and he always skates his hardest. And those qualities have undoubtedly made him one of the all-time most respected skateboarders. —*Joe Hammeke*

Peter Hewitt is a skateboarding original. He rolls faster, grinds harder, and is more exciting to watch than you. If you've seen him ride or have been fortunate enough to skate with him, you know there's not a line he won't find and get his wheels on. Actually, it's hard to find terrain that can even contain the flying rat. He continually pushes the limits of his shred, and his high speed and recklessness are respected by skaters worldwide. It's no wonder he rode for Hosoi back in the day. It seems only natural that he has represented a solid company like Independent for so long. Peter Hewitt rules. I commend his friendship and his dedication to upholding underground traditions. —*Al Partanen*

Clockwise from top sequence: *Going ballistic with a frontal tailgrab 360 at Missile Park in San Diego County, October 1996; Frontside thruster follow-through in the fracture factory tube, Louisville, KY, June 2002; The peanut gallery gets stunned with this youthful stalefish in Carlsbad, CA, June 1991.*

Opposite clockwise from far right: *Peter hits the deck where few dare to grind at Burnside, September 2002; Issuing the crailtap policy at the La Mesa pool, June 2000; Sparky rocks into another Burnside Halloween, 2002.*

"If you've seen him ride or have been fortunate enough to skate with him, you know there's not a line he won't find and get his wheels on."

—Al Partanen

LASEK ✠ ✠ ✠ ✠

"Independent is one of the only companies out there that still has the edge." —Bucky Lasek

When he was a little kid, Bucky Lasek's bike was stolen, so he got interested in skateboarding. Oddly enough, his first board was a Caballero deck, produced by the brand that would eventually become his first major sponsor. Bucky regularly skated the Chesapeake hell ramp and the streets of Baltimore during his upbringing. He was a little grom with skills and determination who used his skateboard as his main source of transportation. Getting to and from skatespots made both street and vert skating a daily routine for him.

Making the transition from being an unknown to a sponsored rider wasn't easy in those days, but Bucky had something special. Tony Hawk could see it during his first encounter with Bucky: "We were in Baltimore on a Bones Brigade tour around 1986, and we kept hearing about a hot young vert skater in town, so we took a trip to the local vert ramp just as it was getting dark. We watched Bucky skate with only car headlights illuminating the ramp and ended up putting him on the Bones Brigade then and there. He was scrawny, but he was able to propel himself without much effort and was trying stuff confidently that was beyond his years." This meeting and subsequent opportunity marked a turning point in Bucky's success and foreshadowed his destiny.

Bucky turned pro with Powell Peralta in 1990, just as vertical skateboarding had ground to a halt in popularity. Bucky was stuck, his dreams vanishing as quickly as they had appeared. Hawk tells it like this: "It was nearly impossible to make a living as a vert skater in the early '90s, and Bucky probably felt like his window of opportunity had closed. I encouraged him to move to California to increase his visibility, but it seemed like a pipe dream to make it as a vert skater in those days. He was also starting a family, so it would have been a major uprooting. He continued to skate, regardless of these circumstances, and he never lost his touch."

Bucky pressed on as best he could and worked at a friend's auto body shop in order to make ends meet. As the '90s hit, skateboarding was at its lowest point in history. Bucky stayed with Powell even after Stacy Peralta left the business and original Bones Brigade members Tony Hawk and Lance Mountain left to start their own companies.

In the years that followed, the US economy grew stronger, and skateboarding began to climb out of its "small wheels and big pants" phase. Hawk, who still believed in Bucky's potential, remembers, "I offered him a position on the Birdhouse team from day one, but he felt more secure at Powell because we were just starting out. He rode for a couple different teams after that, but they went under, and he eventually called me and asked about getting on the team. I had always held a position open for him."

Bucky continued to progress as vert skating picked up momentum. Contests were getting bigger, and special televised events that were normally dominated by the likes of Tony Hawk and others thrived beginning in 1995. Bucky stepped up and won a slew of major championships and televised events and emerged from the 1990s as one of the top dogs on the pro skateboard circuit. He suddenly became extremely popular among young skateboarders, and his success earned him many endorsements and solid sponsorship contracts.

Bucky's dedication to his craft, his competition results, and his video and magazine coverage speak for themselves. But it is his consistent,

Bucky's style and sense of airspace above the lip is absolute; cross-boned lien air at the Encinitas Y, August 1998.

In the realm of a practice session, Bucky whirls a flat spun lien stinger across a wide and ominous chasm at the Boom Boom Huck Jam ramp, January 2003.

technical, and inventive approach to skateboarding that has assuredly fostered the progress of vert skating as a whole and has garnered him high marks from his peers. Bucky claims his favorite trick highlight would have to be landing an Indy 720 to fakie. But, as Hawk puts it, "He can think of a trick and figure it out before he even tries it. Practice is merely incidental."

—K.W., from contributions by Bryce Kanights, Derek Krasauskas, and Tony Hawk

Clockwise from top left: *Caught in the spin cycle of a flat spun backside 540, Bucky holds on for a shot at the podium in Oceanside, CA, October 2002; Mr. Lasek seizes command of a heady corner air at Vans' Combi Pool, May 1999; Backside tailslide in Chula Vista, CA, January 2002; Radiated ollie to fakie high above a subdued smorgasbord of artificial skate terrain, Encinitas, CA, March 2001.*

*Just days after the forms were poured,
Tony literally rocks the cradle at
Port Orford, OR, June 2002.*

tony TRUJILLO

From left: *Eight-wheeled lien to tail in Taupo, New Zealand, December 2002; Terror in Tampa, March 2003; On and off his board, Tony captivates the sea of eyeballs in Marseille, France, May 2002.*

"Tony is, as the saying goes, 'future primitive.' He embodies the past and the future." —Tommy Guerrero

If you've seen Tony Trujillo skate, you know. If you haven't, it's your loss.

Tony started skating when he was six. At age 14, he sent a video with a photo of a huge dildo taped to the cover to Julien Stranger and John Cardiel. "Sponsor me" tapes usually consist of about a minute of one-off tricks. Tony's tape was 20 minutes long, and it was insane. He was a little kid in a snake run, doing huge kickflips followed by Miller flips. It didn't make any sense; his styles crashed together. Old school, new school, fuck that labeling shit … it was 100 percent skateboarding from a teenager who didn't know better or give a shit what anybody thought. This kid was the one, gifted with natural ability, soul, and style. He turned pro when he was 16. What the fuck were you doing when you were 16?

Pure Independent. Built To Grind.

After just a few years as a pro, Tony was up there with the best of all time. He skates like Jay Adams, Mark Gonzales, and Mark Appleyard all rolled into one. Is it a bank? A rail? A skatepark? It doesn't matter, because Tony's got it covered. If it's there, he's skating it. I would eat my right hand to have his lien airs; any other skater would feel the same way. I want for just one day to know what it's like to skate like he does; fuck, it would be great.

Although my severe jealousy about Tony's skating would be dangerous under other circumstances, in this case, it's outweighed by my excitement that there's someone like Tony out there. I'm stoked that the best skaters are still the ones who don't fake it. They feel it, they live it, and they define skateboarding. They will always give us something to shoot for and inspire us to grind longer, go higher, move faster, and get more.

Thank you, Tony. Skateboarding is in good fucking hands. Here's to the future. —*Jim Thiebaud*

"Tony Trujillo makes skating look enjoyable. He flows, he doesn't limit himself, it looks completely natural, and he has no barriers." —Steve Caballero

Although the posted placard doesn't cite skating, TNT lipslides the distance of a stairwell according to nobody's regulations but his own, February 2003.

NO SMOKING DRINKING EATING GRAFFITI

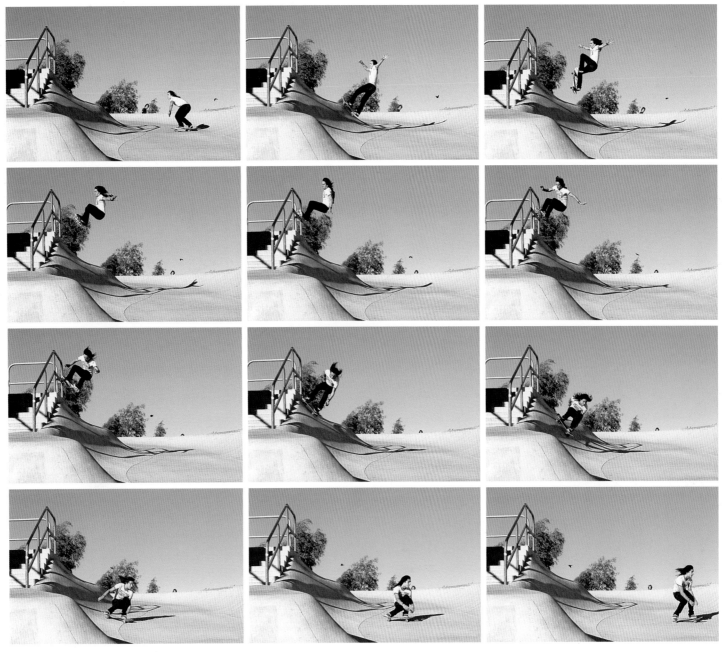

Above: *In a random act of gnarliness, TNT springs up to an inventive grind at Australia's Tuggeranong Skatepark, February 2002.*
Below, from left: *A skate shop demo leads to a fleeting kickflip over a pool of death in Redwood City, CA, July 1999; Tony throws up a proper frontside invert for the young guns in Government Camp, Oregon, August 2001; Skating without pads but with plenty of power and style, Tony sets a fine example of how it's properly done for the next generation in Alameda, CA, July 2000.*

"Trujillo's perfect for representing Independent. You want to ride the trucks just by watching him. The way he skates <u>is</u> Indy." —Andrew Reynolds

STAGE VIII

Original Release Date: September 1998 **Available Sizes:** 126, 136, 146, 156, 166
Other Trucks Available: Stage I 101, Stage IV 215
Available Colors: Silver, Blue Baseplate/Silver Hanger (126 & 136),
Maroon Baseplate/Silver Hanger (126 & 136), Black Baseplate/Silver Hanger (126 & 136)
Features: Added 126 size, Reduced Material on Hanger, Added Cross-Logo Stamp on
Pivot Housing

STAGE VIII
136 mm

STAGE IX

Original Release Date: February 2003
Available Sizes: 129, 139, 149, 159, 169
Other Trucks Available: Stage I 109, Stage IV 215
Available Colors: Silver (All Sizes), Black (129 & 139), Red (129 & 139)
Features: All-New Lightweight Hanger and Baseplate (129 & 139), Upgraded to 4140 Chrome Molly
Steel Axles, Reduced Threads on Axle, New Precision-Drilled Mounting Holes

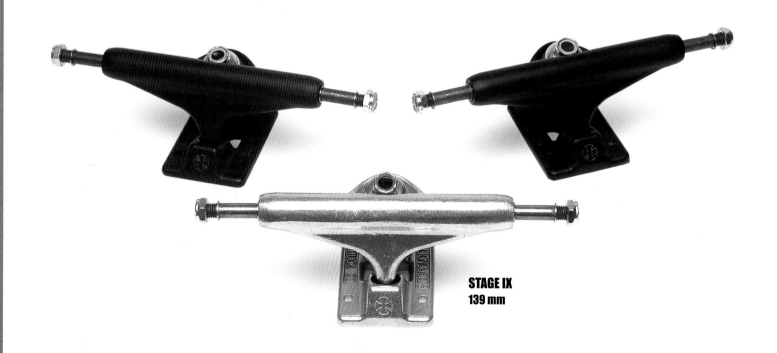

STAGE IX
139 mm

artifacts
1997-2003

• A "Fuck the Rest" team tee, produced in September 2002.

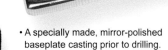

• These two stickers catalog the cross logo's many variations over the years.

• A specially made, mirror-polished baseplate casting prior to drilling.

• A few classic-looking but modern patches, including Beer Label, Built to Grind (with a cross as the "O"), and true words to live by: "Live to Ride, Ride to Live."

• "Hard to Beat" style sheet for T-shirt.

• A sketched concept for trade show display windows promoting the release of the Stage IX truck.

• "Heaven Sent Hell Bent" initial concept sketch for T-shirt, 2003.

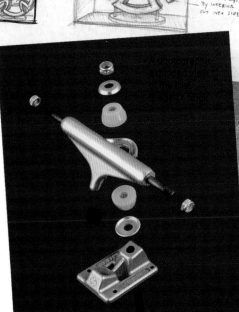

• No, it's not a die-cast toy vehicle, it's an actual Independent Truck Company edition of Ford Motors' Falcon UTE, produced as a contest prize in Australia. On top of its already high-end package features, the vehicle came stock with a grindable roll bar and Independent cross icons throughout the interior and on the wheels and exterior trim.

photo archive
1997-2003

Left: *In a space surely not deemed skateable, Karma Tsocheff throws a shifty over an elemental gap, February 1998. Below: Rob "Sluggo" Boyce latches onto the first-ever backflip on a skateboard via Indy grab at Griffin Skatepark, North Vancouver, BC, October 1997.*

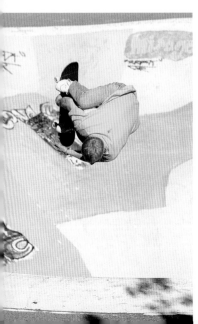

Clockwise from top left: *In the lush confines of Honolulu, the "other" Steve Olson glides through a 180 fakie nosegrind, November 1998; Doug Saenz bashes up a pole that's powerless against his foresight, April 1999; Suspended over a gap, Brian Sumner prepares to Smith grind where others would rather dirty their hands, January 1999; East Coaster Donny Barley grinds to fakie above Sid Abruzzi and his doorway of doom at Skater Island, February 1999.*

#★X!!! HOT!

Royce Nelson

Always hot, Royce Nelson sticks a tailslide at Fresno's renowned Vagabond Pool. Thrasher, February 1998.

> "Even my approach to playing music comes from skateboarding. It's that whole thing of putting yourself out there and not being afraid to try. You just make it happen."
>
> —Ray Barbee

Above: *Josh Falk picks an effective spot to launch a tweaked Indy down a steep San Francisco sidewalk, April 1999.*
Right: *Ray Stevens II punches through a set with The Faction in San Jose, July 2002.* Far right: *A kickflip Indy varial to fakie is one of Mike Crum's many finely tuned weapons, August 2000.*

Opposite: *Miles from paved urbanity and shimmering sidewalks, Jeremy Wray twists a melon grab off the Bristol Salt Flats of Amboy, CA, June 1997.* Above: *While the rails remain knobbed, Brian Anderson opts for taller tactics and locks into this backside tailslide at UCI, July 1999.* Right: *Wear it with pride.*

263

A fair pair of Indy decals, November 1996.

Clockwise from top left: *Al Partanen knocks out a stalefish above crossed shadows at the Clinton Keith Pool, October 2001; Rob Gonzalez slices through the slot with a frontside bluntslide in Barcelona, Spain, August 2001; Tim McKenney crosses a bridge with a drought-driven lien air, Phoenix, Arizona, February 1998; Ethan Fowler puts it all up front on an illuminated nosegrind down a long nine, May 2001.*

Clockwise from top left: *Moses Itkonen stylizes a stretched crooked grind in Vancouver, BC, August 1999; Mikey Chin pounces on the MACBA big four in Barcelona, Spain with a fervent nollie heelflip, July 2002; Moses, a well-known nemesis to security guards worldwide, gets the boot, September 1999; Grindmaster Tony Alva lays into one with eye contact at the Strawberry Pool, July 2002*

Top: *Somewhere in the basement of Utah, Kelly Bellmar reenters a clandestine conduit from the upper quadrant of its elbow, August 2001.*
Left: *A rare and custom-crafted Australian guitar.*

Skip Pronier

INDEPENDENT TRUCK COMPANY

Darren Navarrette

Above: *With wild and controlled actions like these, Darren Navarrette reveals why he's featured and respected on the Indy squad. Slap, June 2000.*
Below: *There's a new sheriff in town, March 2000.*
Right: *Justin Strubing and Tony Cox deliver a pair of decked-out rocks in St. Petersburg, Russia, July 2002.*

Clockwise from top: *Aaron Astorga grinds to fakie along an aquamarine pit, September 2002; Cool cat, July 2001; Jub gets drilled with another illustration of the flesh by Justin Bell at Marks of Art, San Jose, CA, February 2001.*

#★X⚡!!!

And Other Subtle Slogans

Independent ads have always been notorious for making straightforward statements. Some slogans that have appeared over the years:

The Newest and Hottest. Everything Else is Obsolete

That was Then, This is Now

Free on the Streets

Accept no Substitutes

Some Get Air, Others Get High

Speed is the Essence, Stability a Fact

Stop Skate Harassment

Built to Grind

Take No Quarter, Shred All Quarters

All Go, No Show

Paint Walls, Not Trucks

Performance that Has No Equal

Ride the Best, Shine the Rest

Independent Uber Alles

Tools of the Trade

Non Fattening

Seek, Find, and Grind

We Run Our Competition Into the Ground

Performance Proven

Superior in the Streets

No Plastic Allowed

I'd Rather Fight Than Switch

Smoke 'Em

Fools … Don't Ride 'Em

Declaration of Independent

Rise Above the Rest

Free Yourself

Ride the Best, Bust the Rest

Things go Better with Indy

Anytime, Anyplace, Anywhere

Loyalty, Pride, Respect

Punk and Disorderly

Possessed

Ride the Best, Fuck the Rest

#★X⚡!!! YOU!

Revolutionary in its Simplicity

All Other Trucks Suck

By Skaters, for Skaters, Forever

The Backbone of Skateboarding

272

Above: *Kiwi legend Lee Ralph dwarfs an exclusive ramp in San Francisco with a high and mighty Madonna, October 1999.*

Suspended above Burnside's crow's nest, Osage Buffalo flicks seven plys of maple with precision, July 2002.

"We're skateboarders; we'll always change. Whatever is the norm, a skateboarder tries to do the opposite. We're rebellious, like Hell's Angels on wheels. We are the motor on a skateboard." —Mark Gonzales

Constantly digging up original hits, Mark Gonzales threads the needle with unique levitation, October 2000.

An instant before it became a fragment of skateboarding's history, Chet Childress gets the last lick at New Jersey's venerated Asbury Park Pool, October 2002.

Clockwise from above: *During his first visit to Australia's West Coast, Dustin Dollin left his mark on Perth City's exquisite architecture. This backside tailslide to fakie at the Stock Exchange rail is a vivid reminder and has since been skate-stopped, May 2001; Citizen of the world Tony Cox compresses a stale to tail in San Francisco, November 1999; John Igei switch pop shoves over a railing in Berkeley, CA, April 2003; Roll 'em.*

Clockwise from top left: *In the Inland Empire, big snaps provide Reese Forbes a magnificent and distant launch over a loading platform, March 2003; Jen O'Brien floats a backside ollie at the Pala Pool, July 2003; Renowned surf aerialist Christian Fletcher takes to his wheels and reels in a stalefish on European soil, March 2002; Roll 'em again; Christian's son and upcoming young gun, Grayson Fletcher, soars at Ripon Skatepark and upholds the family name, July 2002.*

"Love 'em or leave 'em ... I love 'em, so I'm sticking with Indy." —Darren Navarrette

Above: *Darren Navarrette keeps the effects hot in Tampa, March 2003.* Left: *Neil Heddings gets over the bars, December 2001.*

Opposite page, clockwise from top: *Brazilian Nilton Neves steps to a backside boneless on a functional form, April 2003; "Rival" girls' tee, 2002; Jody McDonald rides and rips for fun at the Ironwood ramp, June 2001.*

Opposite page, clockwise from top left: *In the streets of Los Angeles, Jim Greco stomps a trunk grind between two opposed curbs, December 2002; A crowd of Warped tourists in Melbourne, Australia witnesses the skilled precision of Mike Frazier's effortless front blunts, February 2002; Sam Hitz follows through with a crailslide assault in El Cajon, CA, June 2002; The ink tells it all: Eric D is down for life; His cue in the midst of its tour of duty, September 2003.*

This page: *The tall tales of Joe Pino's super-human ollie abilities are proven true by this episode of parking lot departure, June 2001.*

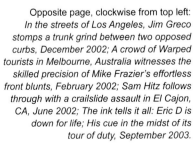

Above: *From the streets of the East, Tino Razo coasts through a frontside boardslide.* Slap, *April 2001.*
Below: *Distinctive and commemorative propaganda for meaningful libations.*

"The skateboarding industry tried to boycott Independent. It was the first time they were confronted with something they could not control. In that, they were correct."

—Fausto Vitello

Clockwise from top left: *Tommy Guerrero stylizes a big ollie at San Francisco's Crocker Amazon Skatepark, October 2001; The true Canadian source of power, Paul Machnau, gaps a distant and overhead jaw-dropper in San Diego, July 2003; On stage with U.S. Bombs, Duane Peters salutes a mob of rockers in San Francisco, April 1998; As gnarly and influential as he's ever been, DP blasts his legendary Indy air at Bellmar's pool, January 2003; Camp Pendleton's troops take notice of Carabeth Burnside's feeble grind before their deployment to the Middle East, April 2003.*

name: *John Hutson*
record: *53.45 mph stand-up downhill*
date: *6.11.78*
location: *Signal Hill, Long Beach, CA*

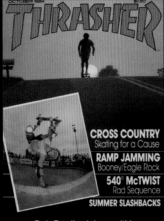

name: *Danny Way*
record: *65' long jump*
date: *4.16.03*
event: *King of Skate*
location: *Temecula, CA*

name: *Bob Denike (along with)*
Jack Smith, Gary Fluitt, Paul Dunn
record: *First four-man team to cross*
America on skateboards
date: *7.1.84–7.26.84*
location: *Newport, OR*
to Williamsburg, VA

name: *Christian Hosoi*
record: *10'6' backside air*
date: *12.14.86*
event: *NSA Pro/Am Finals*
location: *Anaheim Convention Center*
Anaheim, CA

name: *Steve Caballero*
record: *11' backside air*
date: *9.6.87*
location: *Raging Waters*
San Jose, CA

Danny Way's record-setting
board outfitted with a set of
Independent 215s.

name: *Danny Way*
record: *18'3" backside air*
date: *4.17.02*
event: *King of Skate*
location: *Temecula, CA*

name: *Danny Way*
record: *23'5" backside air*
date: *6.12.03*
event: *DC video shoot*
location: *Temecula, CA*

Additional records include:

name: *Christian Hosoi*
record: *Most consecutive ollies*
on vert (69)
date: *5.29.88*
location: *Raging Waters, San Jose, CA*

name: *Danny Way*
record: *13'6" kickflip Indy air*
date: *8.3.97*
event: *Exclusive DC video shoot*
location: *Brown Field, Otay Mesa, CA*

name: *Danny Way*
record: *16'6" backside air*
date: *8.3.97*
event: *Exclusive DC video shoot*
location: *Brown Field, Otay Mesa, CA*

name: *Brian Patch*
record: *58' long jump*
date: *1.23.02*
event: *Guinness Book*
location: *Van Nuys, CA*

name: *Danny Way*
record: *75' long jump (b/s to 360)*
date: *6.12.03*
event: *DC video shoot*
location: *Temecula, CA*

name: *Chad Fernandez*
record: *Longest grind (36'9")*
date: *8.25.03*
event: *Today Show*
location: *New York, NY*

Above: *Bucky Lasek requires a two-page spread to drift a distant frontside rodeo into your face.* Slap, October 2001.
Below left: *The Scott Stamnes Memorial Skate Jam united skaters from all over the planet to ride Orcas Island's flowing forms for the first time. Not one to be left behind, Jimmy "The Greek" Marcus dialed in lines that included this masterful crail on the sauced coping, August 2002. Below right: Clint Peterson evades kinks with a rapidly gapped lipslide in Buenos Aires, Argentina, January 2003.*

Armed with an inverted Indy air, Pete "The Ox" Colpitts crosses the illustrated chasm of doom in Annaka, Japan, May 2003.

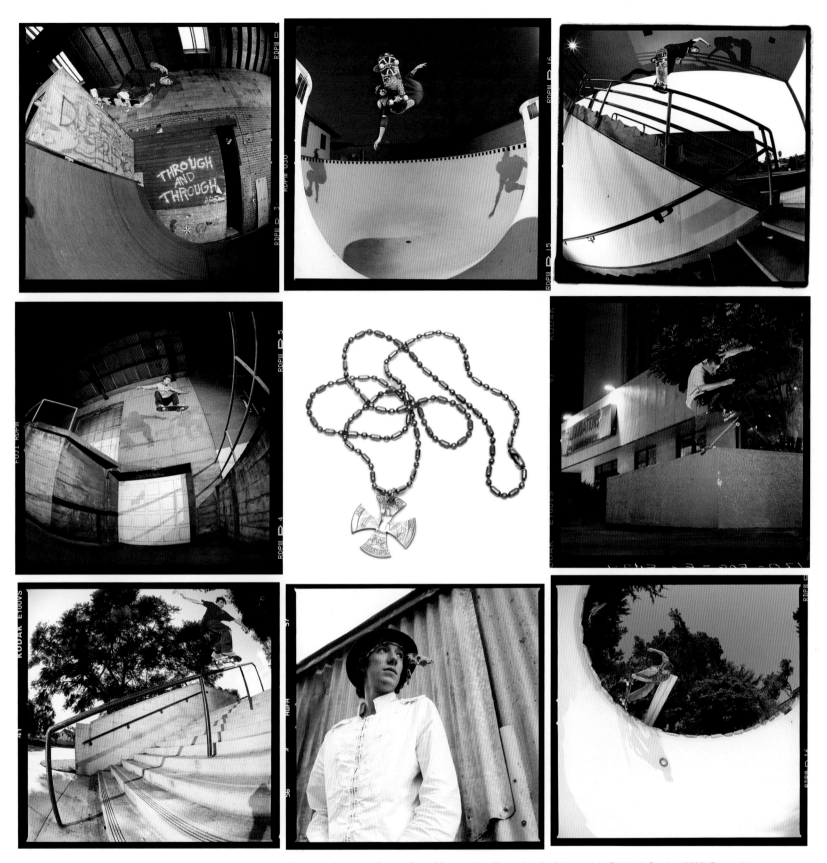

Clockwise from top left: *Max Schaaf flows with agility and crails Jim's ramp in Oakland, October 2002; Darren Navarrette splits the shadows with an ollie to fakie across Bellmar's onion, May 2003; Diego Bucchieri chops through a precarious bluntslide in Los Angeles, June 2001; A nocturnal noseblunt slide in the San Fernando Valley, delivered by Robbie McKinley, October 2000; The rock-encrusted lip of a backyard beauty gets violated by pool mercenary Tony Farmer, August 2002; Ali Boulala kicks it at the Collingwood rubble in Melbourne, Australia, January 2003; Greg Lutzka stretches the landing gear on a backside lipper in California's Inland Empire, May 2002; The simple use of a small hacksaw allows Howard Cooke to leap a large gap in Portland, OR, August 2002. Center: A handmade Maltese/Independent cross charm made by Karina Strangio from a U.S. quarter.*

"All other trucks suck!"

Arto Saari

So true, so true … Arto Saari tells it like it is. Thrasher, June 2001.

Above, from left: *Indy flask reflection of Jake Brown, March 2001; Jake Brown soars into the cloud formations with a torqued lien air at the DC Super Ramp, April 2002.* Below: *The park's celebrated ribbon ceremony was weeks away, but that didn't stop Steve Bailey and his extraordinary ollie Smith grinder in Brookings, OR, December 2001.*

Clockwise from top left: With king-sized style, Aaron Suski reveals why a stalefish should only be done frontside: do it right or don't do it at all, Chandler, AZ, May 2000; Canadian madman Ryan Smith avoids usual security rhetoric and carries out an impervious frontside noseblunt slide at a secretive hubba joint, December 2002; Stacy Lowery drives through a lengthy 5-0 grind in East LA, November 2001; NHS production powerhouse Dave Freil stands trackside with his Indy ride, March 2003.

Top, left to right: *Jani Laitiala pushes through a distant frontside noseslide in his hometown of Helsinki, Finland, August 2001; Alex Moul suspends the flick and catch on this backside flip in Orange County, June 2003.* Below: *A comparative study of the grinding characteristics of two Independent trucks produced and abused 20 years apart. Skateboarding's progress and diverse growth within this time span are visually obvious.*

Above, from left: *Grind where you must. Brian Patch lathers the coping atop an uncommon form in Klammath Falls, OR, September 2003; Young Brazilian dark horse Rodrigo Lima switch nosegrinds in LA County, July 2003. Below, left to right: Doug "Pineapple" Saladino unleashes a frontside double trucker across the lip at Coronado, February 2002; Doug and a buddy in his basket, February 2002.*

"Independent is like a classic muscle car. There's a lot of history associated with it, and many legendary skaters have been part of the program. There are a lot of truck companies out there, but who's dominated as long as Independent has?" —Danny Way

Above: *Seek out new forms of enjoyment; you never know what you may discover.*
Ryan Wilburn reaps the rewards of a backside disaster in Portland, OR, July 2003.
Below right: *Not available to the public, a dealer-only tee, 2003.*

Clockwise from top left: *After bearing a couple decades of inferior truck brand endorsements, Neil Blender comes correct on this eggplant in Clairemont, CA, May 2003; Tony Manfre disregards the brick run up and lets loose on an alluring ledge in Berkeley, CA, April 2003; A winding section of hillside homes blur past Pietot Alcala on a tuck through a tight chicane in San Francisco, October 2003; Three stories up, Sean Stockton stands upon a lengthy 5-0 grind in NorCal, June 2003.*

294

Top: *Austin, TX's Jake Nunn brandishes big guns in the face of an afternoon sun, March 2002.* Above, left to right: *Black Leathermen Olson and Hackett chase and race in San Francisco's Presidio, March 2002; On a new pour at Burnside, the foundations of Dreamland and Grindline Skatepark design teams come into being as Mark Scott and Mark Hubbard work with friends and locals to create their own destiny, October 2001.*

Above: Nicole Zuck pushes it frontside at the Strawberry Lodge bowl, October 2003. Below right: *Dodging the pad police, Peter Hewitt tailgrabs a trajectory into the public pipe in Upland, CA, February 2003.* Below: *Utilitarian by design, the Indy tool belt.* Opposite page, clockwise from top: *Mark Gonzales gets towed by Max Schaaf and then puts the bionic springs into gear to ollie over him, April 2001; Chad Fernandez lipslides an 18-stair gnarler, December 2001; Your grind starts here; Aluminum ingots get the meltdown at Ermico's foundry, September 2003.*

Omar Hassan confirms that many parts of a skatepark are rideable with this precarious and one-of-a-kind backside disaster at Upland, January 2003.

Above, left to right: *Steve Nesser triumphs with a distant pop shove it in Berkeley, CA, 2003; Late-evening ollie tactics with Joey Tershay at the illuminated Pala Pool, September 2002. Below: From the flats, Corey Sheppard locks into a long-ass frontside noseslide and stands tall through six of 11 frames. Slap, September 2002.*

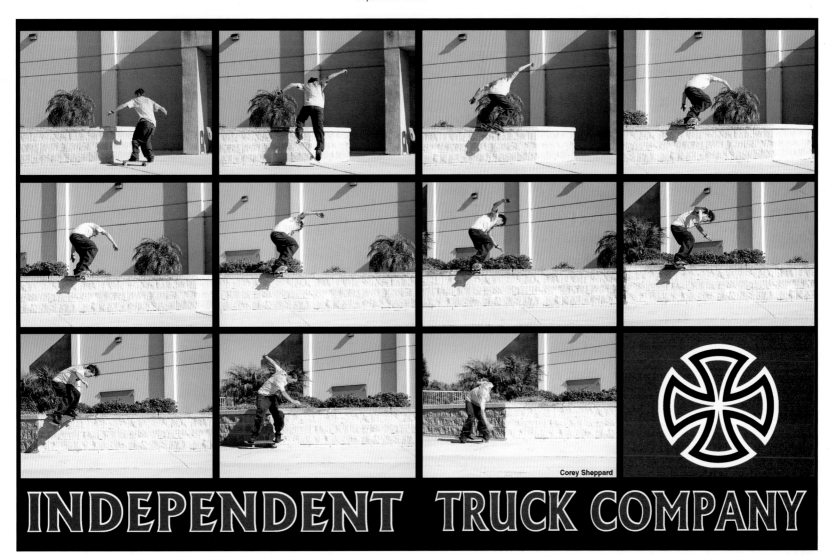

Corey Sheppard

INDEPENDENT TRUCK COMPANY

Javier Mendizibal whips
a backside sugarcane
on the sacred grounds
of the Burnside project,
September 2003.

Clockwise from top left: *Van Wastell propels an extensive crooked grind toward touchdown, August 2003; Running a stylish kit, Ali Boulala lets the bombs drop in Auckland, New Zealand, February 2003; Obscured but not unknown, Kevin "Spanky" Long freshly hucks a stalefish in Berkeley, CA, May 2003; Rob Welsh keeps comfy in his bomb-ass Indy stoner parka, December 2003.*

Continually racking up mind-blowing achievements, Danny Way shamelessly puts a number of pro snowboarders' careers in check with this gapped grinder on his trusty set of 215s. Notice the lack of tail drag. What's next on the hit list? Only Danny knows for sure, September 2003.

Thrasher magazine ▶

1/97 *Lavar McBride* 2/97 *Ben Pappas* 3/97 *Paulo Diaz* 4/97 *Joel Tudor* 5/97 *Pat Channita* 6/97 *Ray Barbee*

7/97 *Karma Tsocheff* 8/97 *Justin Bokma* 9/97 *Omar Hassan* 10/97 *Eric Dressen* 11/97 *Chico Brenes* 12/97 *John Cardiel*

1/98 *Ryan Wilburn* 2/98 *Royce Nelson* 3/98 *Andrew Currie* 4/98 *Tony Miorana* 5/98 *Mark Gonzales* 6/98 *Brian Anderson*

7/98 *Al Boglio* 8/98 *Mike Crum* 9/98 *Rick Blackhart* 10/98 *Diego Bucchieri* 11/98 *Julien Stranger* 12/98 *Andrew Reynolds*

1/99 *Chad Fernandez* 2/99 *Dustin Dollin* 3/99 *Arto Saari* 4/99 *Tony Trujillo* 5/99 *Brad Staba* 6/99 *Danny Supa*

7/99 *Brad Johnson*

8/99 *Aaron Roney*

9/99 *John Cardiel*

10/99 *Tim McKenney*

11/99 *Brian Sumner*

12/99 *Andrew Reynolds*

1/00 *Diego Bucchieri*

2/00 *Judd Hertzler*

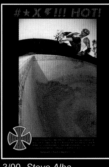

3/00 *Steve Alba*

4/00

5/00 *Biano Bianchi*

6/00 *Bucky Lasek*

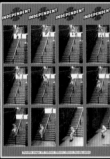

7/00 *Arto Saari*

8/00 *Karma Tsocheff*

9/00 *Rob Gonzalez*

10/00 *Mark Hubbard*

11/00 *Brian Sumner*

12/00 *Tim McKenney*

1/01 *Chet Childress*

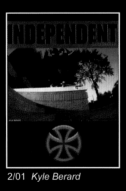

2/01 *Kyle Berard*

3/01 *Joey Pepper*

4/01 *Tony Ferguson*

5/01 *Jake Nunn*

6/01 *Arto Saari*

7/01 *Ali Boulala*

8/01 *Matt Beach*

9/01 *Ryan Smith*

10/01 *Dustin Dollin*

11/01 *Chad Fernandez*

1997-2003 ad archive

12/01 Pat Smith

1/02 Peter Smolik

2/02 Danny Way

3/02 Lee Dansie

4/02

5/02 Aaron Suski

6/02 Blackhart, Peters, Olson, Hackett

7/02 Rob Gonzalez

8/02 Donny Barley

9/02 Marcus McBride

10/02 Ray Barbee

11/02

12/02 Peter Smolik

13/02

1/03 Greg Lutzka

2/03 Mark "Red" Scott

3/03

4/03 Steve Alba

5/03 Danny Supa

6/03 Ed Selego

7/03

8/03 Steve Olson

9/03 Jeremy Wray

10/03 John Cardiel

Slap ▶

11/03

12/03 Ali Boulala

1/97 Mike York

2/97 Andy Roy

3/97 Tommy Guerrero

4/97 Brian Patch

5/97 *Steve Spear*

6/97 *Tim McKenney*

7/97 *Rick Howard*

8/97 *Skip Pronier*

9/97 *Robert Douglas*

10/97 *Satva Leung*

11/97 *Salman Agah*

12/97 *Moses Itkonen*

1/98 *Weston Correa*

2/98 *Curtis Hsiang*

3/98 *Tim Upson*

4/98 *Eric Jay*

5/98 *Pat Channita*

6/98 *Tony Ferguson*

7/98 *Jeff Taylor*

8/98 *Kien Lieu*

9/98 *Joe Sierro*

10/98 *Ryan Wilburn*

11/98 *Marcus McBride*

12/98 *Skip Pronier*

1/99 *Tommy Guerrero*

2/99 *Ben Pappas*

3/99 *Brian Sumner*

4/99 *Pete Colpitts*

5/99 *Matt Beach*

6/99 *Mike Peterson*

7/99 *Ray Barbee*

1997-2003 ad archive

9/99 *Eric Bork*

10/99 *Brad Staba*

11/99 *Chad Fernandez*

8/99 *Airto Jackson*

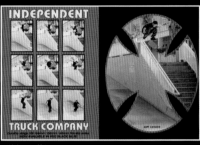

1/00 *Tony Tieu*

2/00 *Josh Falk*

3/00 *Jeff Lenoce*

12/99 *Rob Gonzalez*

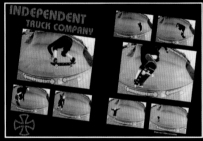

4/00 *Arto Saari*

6/00 *Darren Navarrette*

7/00 *Danny Supa*

5/00 *Brian Sumner*

10/00 *Henry Sanchez*

11/00 *Stacy Lowery*

8/00 *Neil Heddings*

9/00 *Paul Machnau*

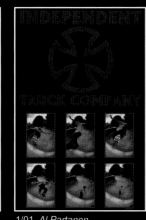

12/00 *Kien Lieu*

1/01 *Al Partanen*

2/01 *Danny Supa*

3/01 *Judd Hertzler*

4/01 *Tino Razo*

5/01 *Mike Maldonado*

6/01 *Neal Mims*

7/01 *Billy Marks*

8/01 *Sean Stockton*

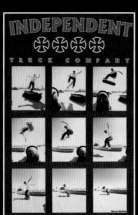

9/01 *Marcus McBride*

10/01 *Bucky Lasek*

11/01 *Alex Moul*

12/01 *Remy Stratton*

1/02 *Paul Machnau*

2/02 *Colin McKay*

Slap ▶

3/02 Wes Lott

4/02 Pat Corcoran

5/02 Chris Roberts

6/02 Peter Hewitt

7/02 Jake Brown

8/02 Alex Gall

9/02 Corey Sheppard

10/02 Steve Bailey

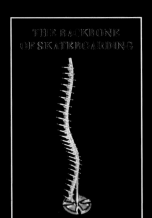
11/02

1/03 Howard Cooke

2/03 Paul Otvos

12/02 Pat Washington

3/03

4/03 *Ryan Wilburn*

5/03 *Jake Nunn*

6/03 *Steve Hernandez*

7/03

8/03 *Clint Peterson*

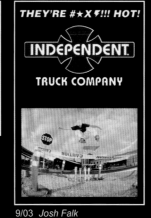

9/03 *Josh Falk*

10/03 *Steve Nesser*

11/03

12/03 *Rob Pluhowski*

1997-2003 ad archive

Long Live the Ride

By Steve Alba

What can be said about a company that has been the raddest skateboard brand going since its inception 25 years ago? Independent Truck Company has outlived all of its rivals and still produces the number-one truck in terms of sales volume and recognition. It has the best and most widely acclaimed logo in the entire skateboarding world and has always attracted the best riders.

By 1977, punk rock was inspiring a new generation of skaters who had not been brainwashed by all-American '70s culture. In its early days, Independent fused the ideals of punk rock and skateboarding into one great pack of misfits and visionaries. They were skaters who hated bellbottom pants, long hair, polyester shirts, black light posters, and all the other crap that the mainstream populace adored during that era. These skaters quickly changed their looks and attitudes to become the movers and shakers of the new revolution. At the forefront of this movement, Independent Truck Company set the pace of things to come with their print ads and brazen riders.

What was instituted 25 years ago has gone on to profoundly affect much of youth culture and mainstream society, which epitomizes everything we originally fought against. Still, the kids nowadays who stoke on Independents do so because the founders laid down the ethical code: skaters in the streets will always do what they want to do. Period. Regardless of how many cities build skateparks, they will never truly succeed. The street skaters will continue finding new spots to practice their art, and the pool skaters will always try to ride every new backyard bonanza that comes their way. What started in the streets will stay in the streets.

In theory, skateboarding is a crime if you stay true to its roots. Trespassing is a part of everyday life for skaters. On a daily basis, they take the heat from the world's non-skaters, and as long as they're experiencing new terrain or improving their skills, they don't think twice about the consequences. These are the dedicated individuals who ride Independent trucks.

Skateboarding is just you and your board. Long live the sessions with your crews, the memories of fallen skate warriors and brethren, all the punkers, the street kids, the pool sharks, the downhill crazies, the old-schoolers, the flippers, the tunnel rats, the simulators, the cone wobblers, and the gnar dogs who all enjoy the freedom of skating under the unwritten law of killing yourself to live. All skaters have to listen to people asking, "You're still riding that wooden toy? When are you going to grow up?" But I realize I will never grow up; skateboarding has forever changed my life. For the better.

"Skateboarding is a crime if you stay true to its roots." —Steve Alba

Fathers and sons, left to right (from opposite page): *Steve Olson tears into a blockbuster carve grind at Mark's Pool in Tahoe City, August 2003; Steve's kid, Alex Parker, hunts down a bluntslide in the evening hours outside of Denver, CO, July 2003; Salba dismisses the loveseat at the Dodger Pool, August 2001; The Alba family bloodline is unmistakable, as little Jesse Wray Alba clocks in above nine o'clock at Upland's public tube, September 2003.*

photo CREDITS

(Pages with multiple credits are listed in clockwise order from top left image.)

Cover
Bryce Kanights

Contents
Page 4-5 Bill Golding

Foreword
Page 6-7 Bryce Kanights
Page 8 Richard Novak, James Cassimus, Bryce Kanights
Page 9 James Cassimus
Page 10-11 James O'Mahoney

Intro
Page 12 John Krisick
Page 13 Reg Caselli, Craig Fineman, Jim Goodrich, Matt Etheridge
Page 14 John Krisick
Page 15 Craig Stecyk, Mörizen Foche, Reg Caselli, NHS, NHS, Tim Piumarta, Jon Malvino, Ed Riggins
Page 16-17 Jerry Alba, John Krisick, Reg Caselli, Bryce Kanights
Page 18-19 Tim Piumarta, James Cassimus, Tim Piumarta, John Krisick, John Krisick
Page 28 Luke Ogden
Page 29 Mörizen Foche, Luke Ogden (truck photo)
Page 30-31 James Cassimus
Page 32 Mörizen Foche, Reg Caselli (all other photos)
Page 33 James Cassimus, Richard Novak, John Krisick, John Krisick
Page 34-35 Greg Cespedes
Page 36 Greg Cespedes
Page 37 Jon Malvino

1978–1981
Page 38-39 James Cassimus
Page 41 Craig Fineman
Page 42 James Cassimus
Page 43 Reg Caselli, James Cassimus, Reg Caselli
Page 44 James Cassimus
Page 45 Kevin J. Thatcher, Ted Terrebonne, Reg Caselli, James Cassimus
Page 46 Craig Fineman, James Cassimus, unknown
Page 47 Craig Fineman
Page 48 Ted Terrebonne, Ted Terrebonne, James Cassimus, Craig Fineman, John Krisick
Page 49 James Cassimus, Craig Fineman
Page 50 Liz Alba, Jerry Alba
Page 51 James Cassimus
Page 52 James Cassimus, James Cassimus, Brad Bowman, James Cassimus
Page 53 Kevin J. Thatcher, James Cassimus, Steve Zirwas
Page 54 Ted Terrebonne
Page 55 Reg Caselli, Reg Caselli, Kevin J. Thatcher
Page 56 Jim Goodrich, Bryce Kanights, James Cassimus, James Cassimus
Page 57 Craig Fineman
Page 60 Reg Caselli (roller skating photo)
Page 62 Jim Goodrich, John Krisick
Page 63 John Krisick
Page 64 Craig Fineman, Craig Fineman, John Krisick
Page 66 Kevin J. Thatcher
Page 67 Craig Fineman
Page 68 Jon Malvino
Page 69 Gary Mederios
Page 70 Craig Fineman
Page 71 Craig Fineman
Page 73 Bryce Kanights, James Cassimus
Page 74 Craig Fineman
Page 75 James Cassimus
Page 76 James Cassimus
Page 78-79 James Cassimus

Page 80 Ted Terrebonne
Page 81 Craig Fineman
Page 82 Ted Terrebonne
Page 84 Ted Terrebonne, Ted Terrebonne, Larry Marshall
Page 85 Craig Fineman
Page 86 Craig Fineman, Reg Caselli
Page 87 Kevin J. Thatcher
Page 88 Kevin J. Thatcher, Ted Terrebonne, Reg Caselli, Rich Rose
Page 90 Reg Caselli, Kevin J. Thatcher
Page 91 Jack Folmer, Reg Caselli, Mörizen Foche
Page 95 Jay Shuirman painting, courtesy of Jim Phillips

1982–1986
Page 96-97 Mörizen Foche
Page 98 Mörizen Foche
Page 99 Mörizen Foche, Rich Rose, Mörizen Foche
Page 100 J. Grant Brittain
Page 101 Kevin J. Thatcher, Kevin J. Thatcher, Cesario Montaño
Page 102 Bryce Kanights, Cesario Montaño, J. Grant Brittain, J. Grant Brittain
Page 103 Tod Swank, J. Grant Brittain, J. Grant Brittain
Pages 104-107 Bryce Kanights
Page 108 J. Grant Brittain, J. Grant Brittain, Bryce Kanights
Page 109 Mörizen Foche
Page 110 J. Grant Brittain, Bryce Kanights, Mörizen Foche
Page 111 J. Grant Brittain
Page 116 Mörizen Foche
Page 117 Mörizen Foche, Matt Etheridge, Mörizen Foche, Bryce Kanights, Mörizen Foche, Mörizen Foche
Page 118 Mörizen Foche, Reg Caselli, Reg Caselli
Page 119 Mörizen Foche
Page 120 Matt Etheridge
Page 121 Jeff Newton, Mörizen Foche, Mörizen Foche
Page 123 Mörizen Foche, Matt Etheridge, Matt Etheridge, Bryce Kanights
Page 124-125 Bryce Kanights
Page 126-127 Mörizen Foche
Page 128 Matt Etheridge, Matt Etheridge, Mörizen Foche, Matt Etheridge
Page 130 Mörizen Foche
Page 131 Bryce Kanights
Page 132 Mörizen Foche Bryce Kanights, Bryce Kanights, Mörizen Foche
Page 133 Bryce Kanights
Page 134 J. Grant Brittain, Bryce Kanights, Bryce Kanights
Page 136 J. Grant Brittain
Page 137 Steve Keenan, J. Grant Brittain, J. Grant Brittain, J. Grant Brittain
Page 138 Mörizen Foche

1987–1990
Page 142-143 Chuck Katz
Page 144 Kevin J. Thatcher, Bryce Kanights, Mörizen Foche
Page 145 Chris Ortiz
Page 146 J. Grant Brittain, Mörizen Foche, Steve Keenan, Bryce Kanights
Page 147 Bryce Kanights, J. Grant Brittain, Mörizen Foche, J. Grant Brittain
Page 148 J. Grant Brittain, Kevin J. Thatcher, Luke Ogden
Page 149 Chuck Katz
Page 150 J. Grant Brittain, Bryce Kanights, Chuck Katz, J. Grant Brittain
Page 151 J. Grant Brittain
Page 152 Joe Brook, Thomas Campbell, Luke Ogden
Page 153 Luke Ogden
Page 154 Jon Humphries, Luke Ogden, Jon Humphries
Page 155 Luke Ogden, Mark Whiteley, J. Grant Brittain
Page 158 Aaron Sedway
Page 159 Bryce Kanights
Page 161 Bryce Kanights
Page 162 Luke Ogden
Page 163 Luke Ogden, J. Grant Brittain, Mörizen Foche
Page 165 Mörizen Foche, Keith Stephenson, Florian Böhm
Page 166 Miki Vuckovich

314

During the many months of book production, our friend and contributing photographer Craig Fineman passed away after a long-term illness. We sincerely appreciate his generous and significant contribution of photographs to this project.

The list of names on the front and back end papers of this book represent a combination of current and former team riders and people that have been involved with Independent over the years. Some of the team riders listed no longer ride for Independent but their contributions to the brand have not gone unnoticed. For those of you that we forgot, we apologize. Thank you.

Unsung Heroes ✠ ✠ ✠ ✠

It's not the board—painted, stained, and pressed; cracked, chipped, and chunked; delaminated, flat, or warped. Though the actual piece of wood is the first thing that comes to mind when we think of our pastime, it's still not the board.

It's not the wheels, that rolling foursome, that ménage à trois plus one. Though they are what connect us to the streets, it's only a matter of time before they're coned, flatspotted, and yellowed. As the most toxic part of the setup, the wheels are doomed at birth to permanent residence in a toxic landfill. So it's not the wheels.

It's not the bolts. The bolts—stripped, bent, rattled, and broken—rarely make it to the next setup. It's not the griptape, designed for only one-time usage. Like the relationship between a parasite and its host, griptape is hopelessly dependent on the life span of the board.

It's not the bearings—rusted, popped, and spent. Bearings are by far the most temperamental component of our ride.

It's not a riser pad, a skid plate, a nose guard, a nosebone, a tailbone, or a set of rails. Who uses those anymore? And it's certainly not your stickers.

It's the trucks that are the unsung heroes of the skateboard. It's the trucks that embody what skateboarding is all about: perseverance, simplicity, and the ability to turn.

Trucks are, quite literally, heavy metal—born in fire and poured like molten lava into a cast that is destroyed, never to be used again. Jolted by axle stalls, torqued by crooked grinds, and pinched by our heavy landings, they put up a mean fight on our behalf.

The trucks are the most difficult thing on a skateboard to break; they're the last man standing. On a contraption designed to be destroyed, they offer the only glimmer of longevity. Like a bottle of good Merlot, they get better with age. Even the hardcore skater can ride, and will willingly ride, the same set for years. The most precisely engineered part of the skateboard, the trucks shy away from excess. As a result of both fashion and function, minimal décor has always been the rule of thumb. Flashiness is neither needed nor welcomed.

The essence of skateboarding—movement—is in the trucks. True, it's the bearings and wheels that allow us to roll, but only in a straight line. It's the trucks that allow us to turn. They're what make skateboarding three-dimensional. Trucks are what transform getting from point A to point B into getting from point A to point Z.

The trucks are the ultimate observers of our triumphs and our follies. They've witnessed our first stair jump, the first time we hit the coping, and our first flip trick. They've recorded our slams, our bails, and our hang-ups. The stories are objectively etched into the hangers as traces of the red curb that was just slappied, the chips of blue paint from the rail that was just 5-0'd, and the murky water from the puddle that was just splashed through—remnants of our recent past. They tell no lies.

For your dedication, your fluidity, and your strength—and because the best way to get out some aggression is with a grind—trucks, this one's for you. —*Aaron Meza,* Skateboarder *magazine, July 2003, Volume 12, No. 11*

DENT	KEVIN O'REGAN	JIMMY MARCUS	SERGIE VENTURA	JOHN STEPHENSON	SCOTT DUNLAP	JAY HAIZLIP
RODRIGO LIMA	NEIL HEDDINGS	BIANO BIANCHI	ANTHONY HANCOCK	ERIC JAY	DUSTIN DOLLIN	
GRIND	SHAWN MARTIN	FRANK IWANICKI	TROY CLOWER	TROY MILLER	JASON LEE	MICKE ALBA
GREG AGUILAR	JIM MURPHY	PHIL LADJANSKI	GAVIN O'BRIEN	MAX SCHAAF	STACY LOWERY	B
DENT	JASON ROGERS	MOFO	DOUG SALADINO	JOHN GIBSON	LORI RIGSBY	MATT DYKE
RYAN WILBURN	CHUCK WAMPLER	KELLY ROSECRANS	CHRIS LIVINGSTON	DOUG SMITH	MATT RODRIGUEZ	
GRIND	MARC HOLLANDER	JASON TAYLOR	SEAN STOCKTON	CRAIG NEJEDLY	DAVE CRIDDLE	JOHN SWOPE
MIKE SMITH	PAULO DIAZ	JESSE MARTINEZ	DAVID ZAKRZEWSKI	PAT CHANNITA	REGGIE BARNES	B
DENT	TIM JACKSON	CHAD SHETLER	CHRIS BORST	NOAH SALASNEK	PAUL WISNIEWSKI	CLAUS GRABKE
PIERRE BENITOMAKO	JORDAN RICHTER	JOEY TRAN	BILLY DEANS	ROB ROSKOPP	NEAL MIMS	
GRIND	JEFF HEDGES	JOANNE GILLESPIE	DAVE HACKETT	JOEL TUDOR	TIM MCKENNEY	ANDY HOWELL
BILLY WALDMAN	MARK SAITO	JIM GRECO	FRANK LANNON	SALMAN AGAH	RICK IBASETA	B
DENT	GEOFF ROWLEY	JOEY PEPPER	RANDY KATEN	LANCE MOUNTAIN	DANNY SARGENT	JIM MARTINO
ROD SAUNDERS	TONY GUERRERO	SEAN YOUNG	DAVID PALMER	STEVE STEADHAM	CHUCK HULTS	
GRIND	AARON MURRAY	CARL SHIPMAN	GABRIEL RODRIGUEZ	RONNIE BERTINO	EDDIE ELGUERA	DAN ZIMMER
CHET THOMAS	KYLE BERARD	ROB WELSH	TREY WINSLOW	RICKY OYOLA	BARRY DECK	BL
DENT	CHRIS ROBERTS	VAN WASTELL	CHRIS ROBISON	JOHN FABRIQUER	SCOTT SMILEY	ADAM MCNATT
RICHARD PAEZ	KARMA TSOCHEFF	TERRY BROWN	GRANT TAYLOR	STEVE NESSER	CLINT PETERSON	
GRIND	RICH LOPEZ	JAY SMITH	STEVE SPEAR	RICKY STILES	CHRIS BAUCOM	ALEX MOUL
REMY STRATTON	MATT PAILES	GARY CROSS	CHAD MUSKA	BEN GILLEY	DARREN NAVARRETTE	BL
DENT	TONY PEREZ	ROBBIE MCKINLEY	JOE SIERRO	SEAN ANDREWS	JOE FONG	MIKE KRESKY